CU00683798

Introduction to Interest-Rate Risk

INTRODUCTION TO
INTEREST-RATE RISK

Brian Coyle

FINANCIAL
WORLD
Publishing
THE CHARTERED INSTITUTE OF BANKERS

Apart from any fair dealing for the purpose of research or private study, or criticism or review, as permitted under the Copyright, Designs and Patents Act 1988, this publication may be reproduced, stored or transmitted, in any form or by any means, only with the prior permission in writing of the publisher, or in the case of reprographic reproduction in accordance with the terms and licences issued by the Copyright Licensing Agency. Enquiries concerning reproduction outside those terms should be addressed to the publisher's agents at the undermentioned address:

Financial World Publishing
IFS House
4-9 Burgate Lane
Canterbury
Kent
CT1 2XJ
United Kingdom

Telephone: 01227 818687

Financial World Publishing publications are published by
The Chartered Institute of Bankers, a non profit making registered educational charity.

The Chartered Institute of Bankers believes that the sources of information upon which this book is based are reliable and has made every effort to ensure the complete accuracy of the text. However, neither CIB, the author nor any contributor can accept any legal responsibility whatsoever for consequences that may arise from errors or omissions or any opinion or advice given.

Typeset by Kevin O'Connor
Printed in Italy

© The Chartered Institute of Bankers 2001

ISBN 0-85297-439-6

Contents

Introduction to Risk

Risk is the possibility that future events might turn out badly, or that something undesirable might happen. Risk is categorized according to what might go wrong, such as the risk of fire, burglary or personal injury. It is also quite common, especially in business, to give types of risk a name, as a shorthand form of description. Health risk, for example, is readily understood to mean the risk that something will happen to cause illness or bad health.

Business Risk and Financial Risk

Risk in business is the possibility that an organization's operations will deteriorate, so that future results will be worse than predicted or expected. Companies face two broad types of risk, business risk and financial risk.

- Business risk arises when a company's commercial activities and operations are less successful than in the past or than expected. For example, sales turnover might fall because a competitor undercuts a company's prices, or introduces a rival product. It is well-recognized that the function of management is to meet the challenges of business risk and bring successful products and services to market in an efficient and effective way.
- Financial risk is perhaps less understood. It is the risk that financial conditions could be either less favourable than expected, or could change causing the business position to deteriorate. Financial conditions relate to money and debts,

such as the cost of borrowing, the yield from investments, the availability of money to borrow and customer bad debts.

Financial risk can be divided into:

- credit risk
- currency risk
- country risk
- interest rate risk.

Credit Risk

Credit risk is the possibility that customers who have been granted credit will either fail to pay when payment is due, or will delay payment and take longer credit than agreed. Failure to pay is a bad-debt risk that has a direct impact on profits. Delayed payments from customers also create a cost, however, because money is still owed that ought to be cash in the bank, either reducing a bank overdraft or earning interest on deposit.

Currency Risk

Currency risk involves losses from adverse movements in foreign exchange rates, both short-term and long-term. It affects any company that sells abroad or buys from abroad in foreign currency, or that has foreign subsidiaries. Indirectly, it also affects any company that has foreign competition in its domestic markets.

Example
A UK company agrees to buy equipment from a US supplier at a price of $144,000. It will take two months to deliver the equipment and the company will then take a further two months' credit. The sterling/dollar exchange rate at the date of the purchase agreement is £1 = $1.60, so the expected purchase cost in sterling is £90,000 (144,000 ÷ 1.60).

Analysis

From the date of the purchase agreement to the date of payment, there is an exposure to currency risk, because of the possibility of an adverse change in the sterling/dollar exchange rate. When payment for the equipment is due, the dollar might have strengthened in value to £1 = $1.50, for example, and the company's cost in sterling would then be £96,000 (144,000 ÷ 1.50), or £6,000 higher than originally expected.

The long-term competitiveness of domestic companies against foreign rivals is also at risk from adverse changes in the exchange rate. For example, a US producer and a UK producer might manufacture an identical item for $3 and £2 respectively. If the exchange rate is £1 = $1.50, the two companies would be manufacturing the product at exactly the same cost. Suppose however that the dollar fell in value to £1 = $2. The item the US company is still producing for $3 would then be much cheaper than the item the UK company is producing for £2. The change in the exchange rate would in this instance give the US producer a distinct advantage in cost-competitiveness that it could exploit to the disadvantage of its UK rival in the US, the UK and other markets.

Country Risk

Country risk arises from an adverse change in the financial conditions of a country in which a business operates. There are three aspects of country risk.

- *Political risk.* This is the risk of deteriorating financial conditions from the consequences of a change of government or political regime, or from continuing uncertainty about what a government might do. The risk is greatest in countries with political instability, because a change in government could be sudden and the actions of the incoming government unpredictable and drastic, e.g. the imposition of exchange controls, nationalization of the banks etc.

- *Regulatory risk.* This is the risk that regulations affecting financial conditions will be introduced, or that existing regulations will be enforced more severely than in the past. One such example would be the risk of harsher regulations about the minimum deposits commercial banks must maintain with the central bank.
- *Economic risk.* This is the risk that economic conditions within a country will have harmful financial consequences, particularly for inflation, interest rates and foreign-exchange rates. If a government were to decide, for example, to increase spending by borrowing heavily, business opportunities would arise for suppliers and contractors to the government, but the financial consequences of a larger government spending deficit (excess of expenditure over income that must be financed by government borrowing) might be much higher interest rates for commercial and private borrowers.

Interest-Rate Risk

Interest-rate risk arises from adverse changes in interest rates, causing higher interest costs or lower investment income, and therefore lower profits or even losses. The risk exists for any business that borrows funds or invests, short-term or long-term, in interest-bearing assets such as gilts, bonds or money-market deposits.

Much medium-term or long-term borrowing and lending is at a floating rate of interest, with the rate payable or receivable reset periodically at review dates (rollover dates or reset dates) when it is adjusted to current market rates. Fixed-rate investments such as most bonds, pay a fixed coupon rate on the face value of the investment, but their *market* value rises or falls in response to changes in the current market rate of interest, giving the investor a capital gain or loss accordingly.

Categories of Financial Risk

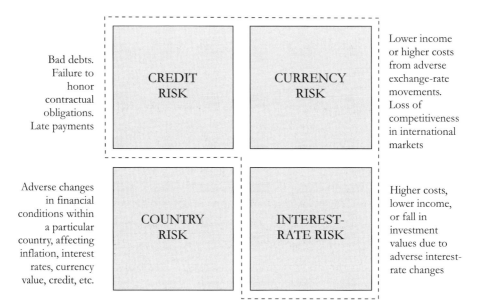

These categories of financial risk are all interrelated. For example, exchange-rate stability (currency risk) in a country with a weak economy (country risk) might be achievable only with higher interest rates (interest-rate risk), increasing the possibility of bad debts for business (credit risk).

Other Categories of Financial Risk

Financial risk can be categorized in other ways, and you may come across a variety of risk terms. Some are listed below.

- *Price risk*. This is the risk that the market price or value of a security, such as a bond, might fall. In the case of interest-bearing securities, price risk arises from the risk of changes in market rates of interest, and from the risk of a deterioration in the credit quality of the issuer of the securities, i.e. the borrower.
- *Market risk*. This is another term for price risk, and refers to an exposure to the possibility of an adverse price change for an item in the market.

- *Liquidity risk.* This refers to the possibility that the market for a security, such as a bond or stock, might be illiquid, so that holders of the security could have difficulty in selling their holding easily, should they wish to do so, at a fair price.

Exposures to Financial Risk

An exposure is a term meaning the existence of risk. Exposures normally can be measured and quantified.

- An exposure to credit risk occurs whenever a business grants credit to a customer. The size of the exposure is the amount owed. Credit lasts until the customer pays.
- An exposure to currency risk (a currency-transaction exposure) occurs whenever a business sells or buys in a foreign currency, and the exposure is the expected amount of currency income or payments. It lasts until the income is received and converted into domestic currency, or the payment is made.
- An exposure to interest-rate risk occurs whenever a business borrows or invests or lends money at a rate of interest. The amount of the exposure is the amount borrowed, invested or lent, and the exposure lasts until the loan is repaid or the investment ceases.

Exposures to financial risk from particular transactions are temporary, and will last until the transaction is completed. Exposures to risk from holding an investment will last as long as the investment is retained. Organizations making financial transactions regularly, or acquiring and disposing of investments regularly, will have continual exposures, with existing exposures coming to an end but with new exposures being created.

With many transactions and financial instruments, more than one type of financial risk is involved. For example, suppose that a Spanish bank holds dollar-denominated fixed-interest bonds, issued by the government of a developing country. The financial exposures of the Spanish bank will be:

- to currency risk: a fall in the value of the dollar against the euro will reduce the value of the bonds *in euros* (the bank's domestic currency), thereby creating a loss for the purpose of financial reporting by the bank
- to interest-rate risk: a rise in US interest rates will reduce the market value of the bonds in dollars, and so result in losses for the Spanish bank
- to credit risk: the bond issuer might fail to pay interest on the bonds when it falls due, or might fail to redeem the bonds at maturity.

Example

During a period in the mid 1990s, the dollar slumped in value against the Japanese yen, falling from an exchange rate of over 100 yen to the dollar to a rate of about 80 yen to the dollar. Interest yields on dollar investments were much higher than on yen-denominated investments. A consideration for Japanese investors at the time would have been whether to invest in yen-denominated investments yielding a negligible return, or to invest in dollar instruments for a higher interest yield, but accept the risk that the value of the dollar investments in yen might fall if the dollar continued to slump in value. For a time, it would have been better for Japanese investors to buy yen investments, even though the yield was very small, because the interest yield on dollar investments would have been more than offset by the loss caused by the collapse in the dollar's value. Japanese investors in dollar fixed-interest investments would, for a time, have suffered negative overall returns.

Higher interest rates are often associated with weak currencies, because a high rate of interest is needed to persuade foreign investors to hold assets in a weak currency and accept the risk of losses due to a fall in the currency's value. However, high interest rates and a weak currency do not necessarily go hand in hand. For example, in the year and a half after the launch of the euro in January 1999, the exchange-rate value of the euro against the dollar fell from nearly 1.20 dollars to the euro, to not much more than 80 cents to the euro. Although the euro demonstrated much weakness against the dollar during this period, interest rates on the euro were lower than on dollar-denominated investments. In other words, investors in dollar securities benefited from both higher yields and a higher rate of interest than investors in euro-denominated securities.

Two-way Nature of Financial Risk

The word exposure suggests perhaps that the outcome of a risk always will be adverse whenever financial conditions change. In reality, however, financial risk is often the possibility that actual results will be either better or worse than expected. Conditions could change favorably, increasing income or reducing costs and adding to a company's profitability. Interest rates could go down for the borrower or up for the investor and lender. The level of bad debts could fall below expectation. Exchange rates could move in a company's favor, rather than adversely.

The problem with risk, however, is that although future profits could benefit if circumstances were to change favorably, an adverse change might have serious consequences for the future of the business. For example, a company borrowing $5 million at a floating rate of interest would benefit from a 3% p.a. fall in interest rates, saving $150,000 each year. In contrast an increase in interest rates by the same amount could create losses or place an unsustainable burden on the company's cash flow. Many companies regard financial risk management as prudent, if not essential, to protect themselves from the risk of adverse changes in financial conditions.

Risk Management

When financial risk is perceived to be high, management might wish to take measures to reduce or contain it. Taking measures to reduce risk or remove risk is known as hedging the risk.

A risk-averse company will seek to minimize its financial risks. Although better-than-expected outcomes would be very welcome, a seriously worse-than-expected outcome could result in unaffordable losses. Risk-management strategies therefore might require a company to restrict potential upside gains in order to limit the potential downside losses. It is the consequence of worse-than-expected results, the downside risk, that management seeks to limit.

One form of risk management is insurance. An insurer can estimate the probability of an event happening and by building up a sufficient volume of business by selling insurance policies, can spread the risk, allowing individual customers to obtain risk insurance for the cost of a premium. Insurance reduces the risk for the buyer and the buyer is willing to pay the cost of the premium for this protection, even though many policyholders never need to make a claim, or have claims that fall short of the premiums they have paid. A number of instruments available for hedging financial risk, such as interest-rate options, work on a similar principle.

When to Manage Interest-Rate Risk

Interest-rate risk affects companies that borrow or lend money, exposing them to higher interest costs or lower interest income, reducing profits. The size of the exposure depends on the company's funding or investment requirements. The scale of the risk depends partly on the size of the exposure, but also on the duration of the exposure, and the risk of adverse interest-rate movements in the period of the exposure.

Interest-rate risk management is most appropriate for banks, financial institutions and companies that borrow or invest quite heavily. For example, a company making an acquisition will experience a dramatic change in interest-rate exposure in a short time if the acquisition is funded by borrowing rather than by issuing shares. It might also suffer a deterioration in creditworthiness or to its credit rating. For example, this happened to a number of telecommunications companies in Europe during 2000, after borrowing to finance acquisitions or to finance the purchase of third-generation telecommunications licenses.

For a company with large debts, the objective should be to achieve the lowest cost of funds. This does not mean borrowing at the lowest current rate available necessarily, because there may be a risk from adverse interest-rate changes in the future.

Banks and other financial institutions, with large amounts of interest-earning assets such as loans and investments, as well as interest-bearing liabilities, usually have large interest-rate exposures. These must be managed to ensure that the bank or institution earns satisfactory and stable profits regardless of interest-rate movements.

Inefficient management of the interest-rate risk on investments is an opportunity loss that reduces profitability. Inefficient management of interest-rate risk for a heavily borrowed company can represent the difference between survival and bankruptcy.

Interest-Rate Exposures

Interest-rate risk has been defined as the risk to profits from adverse changes that might occur in interest rates, resulting in higher interest costs, a fall in investment income or income from lending, or a change in the market price of financial securities.

Changes in Interest Rates

Interest rates can change in various ways.

- The general level of interest rates could go up or down.
- Relative interest rates could change. Interest rates on some financial instruments could change in relation to interest rates on other financial instruments. For example, the rate on a three-month bank deposit could rise by a quarter of a per cent (25 basis points) when the rate on a three-month corporate loan note might rise, for example, by just 3/16ths of one per cent (18.75 basis points).
- There could be a change in the *yield curve* (the term structure of interest rates) so that short-term interest rates change in relation to long-term interest rates. For example, short-term rates could fall while long-term interest rates rise. Alternatively, short-term rates could rise by 2% p.a. whereas long-term rates rise by just 1%.

There are four aspects of risk arising from such rate changes.

- The risk of higher interest charges or lower investment income than anticipated, because of a movement up or down in the general level of interest rates.

- The risk that a borrowing decision will not achieve the lowest possible interest costs because of the way that interest rates move after the decision has been made.
- The risk that a lending or investment decision might be made that, in retrospect, will not have yielded the greatest income, because of the way in which interest rates have moved since the decision was taken.
- The risk of a fall in the price of an interest-sensitive security held as an investment, because of an adverse movement in the interest rate. (Interest-sensitive securities include any securities that provide an interest return to their owner, such as bonds, bills, certificates of deposit, and so on.)

Judgment is important in deciding *how, when* and for *how long* to borrow or invest.

Changes in the General Level of Interest Rates

Companies that borrow, lend or invest are exposed to any adverse movements in the general level of interest rates. A rise in interest rates would mean higher charges for variable-rate borrowers. Lower interest rates would reduce the income from variable-rate investments.

Since most medium-sized and small companies can borrow only at a variable rate of interest, these borrowers will be exposed to the risk of a rise in interest rates. Their interest-rate exposure is the full amount of their borrowed funds.

A distinction can be made between the risk from higher interest rates for borrowers and the broader risks (including interest-rate risk) that arise from high financial gearing in a company's capital structure.

Example

A large public company with borrowings of $500 million expects to make a profit before interest of $100 million. The borrowing is all at a variable interest rate, currently 10%, and the expected profit after interest is $50 million. If business risk is high, because of strong competition for example, sales could be disappointing and actual profit before interest could be only $40 million, leaving the company unable to pay its interest charges because of its high debt level. The company's real problem in this situation is the state of its business, a problem compounded by a high debt burden.

Suppose instead predicted sales and profits before interest are achieved but that *interest-rate risk* is high. Interest rates might rise to 14%, increasing the company's annual charges to $70 million and reducing the profit after interest to just $30 million. This profit loss is a direct consequence of interest-rate risk, without any business risk element attributing to the decline.

This distinction can be useful because in the recent past, there have been many well-publicized failures of heavily indebted companies. To some extent, the problems of these companies were created by high interest rates, but a larger part of their problems resulted from disappointing business conditions, poor sales or high expenditures. The consequences of interest-rate risk, however, can add to the effect of poor trading conditions when rates rise and help to push companies towards collapse. Interest rates alone are not usually the root problem of a company's difficulties, but rather the final event that leads to disaster.

There have been instances also of companies with profitable trading operations becoming insolvent because of the weight of their interest payment obligations.

Interest Rates and Price Risk

Investors in bonds are exposed to price risk after adverse movements or expectations of adverse movements, in interest rates.

The mathematics of pricing fixed interest bonds is not explained in this text. Briefly, however:

- when interest rates rise or are expected to rise shortly, bond prices will fall
- when interest rates fall or are expected to fall shortly, bond prices will rise.

Interest-Rate Risk: General Level of Interest Rates

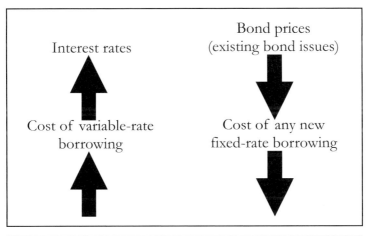

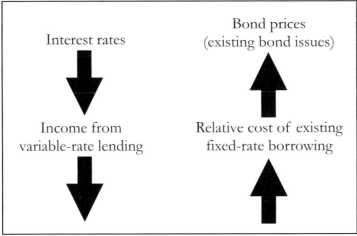

Suppose for example that long-dated US Treasury bonds with a coupon rate of 6% p.a. have a market price of $100. This means that the price of the bond in the market is $100 for bonds with a face value (nominal value) of $100. Investors therefore are willing to pay $100 in return for obtaining annual interest payments of $6, and the repayment of the face value of the bond ($100) when the bond eventually matures. The mathematics are not shown here, but the yield to the investor on the bond is 6%.

Now suppose that interest rates in the market rose from 6% to 8%. Bond investors will now require a higher yield on their investments than previously, and the market price of the 6% US Treasury bond will fall. Receiving annual interest of $6 per $100 (face value) of bonds is no longer sufficient to justify a market price of $100. The market price of the bond will fall to a level where investors buying the bonds in the market will obtain a yield of 8% on their investment. (The market price could fall as low as $75 (= $100 × 6%/8%) but the actual fall in price also will depend on the length of time to the redemption of the bond, when the investor will receive a redemption payment of $100 per $100 face value of bonds.)

Any investor in fixed-rate bonds, or any bank holding bonds for dealing purposes, is constantly exposed to price risk from the possibility of higher interest rates, and even *expectations* of higher interest rates.

In 1994, a number of US and UK banks reported disappointing trading results in their first half-year. In some cases, much of the reason for their disappointing performances was attributed to losses on bond trading. Early in the year, interest rates had risen unexpectedly. Banks holding large quantities of fixed interest bonds therefore recorded losses on revaluing them to their new, lower market value. For example, if a bank held bonds with a market value of $100 million, and the value of the bonds fell to $95 million, the bank would be required to report a loss on its bond trading of $5 million, even if it simply held the bonds and did not sell them.

Interest-Rate Risk and Credit Standing

A company borrowing at a variable rate from a bank is at risk to a higher general level of interest rates, and also to a change in the bank's perception of the company as a credit risk. If the borrower's credit status declines, lenders will ask for a higher rate of interest in new lending agreements to compensate for the greater credit risk.

Example

In the UK in 1991, interest rates (the base rates of commercial banks) fell by 350 basis points, from 14% to 10.5%. A number of companies were reported to be surprised and annoyed that interest rates on their variable rate bank loans did not fall by nearly the same amount. It was suggested that the banks were keeping the benefit of lower market rates to themselves instead of passing it on to customers. Banks responded by saying that the creditworthiness of some customers had been reassessed in view of the depressed economic conditions at the time, and interest rates were now being charged on their loans at a higher margin above the base rates than before. Thus a company might have paid 4% over base when the base rate was 12%, but 6% over base when the rate fell to 10.5%, with the result that the interest on its loan would have gone up from 16% to 16.5% despite the general fall in market rates.

Example 2

The same problem can affect companies that borrow directly from investors by issuing bonds, notes or commercial paper.

A company might establish a commercial-paper (CP) program, whereby it can raise short-term funds by selling CP to investors. CP is a form of debt that the company promises to repay at maturity. It is purchased at a price below its face value, and redeemed by the issuer at par (face value) at maturity. The size of the discount (the difference between the discounted issue price and the redemption price) reflects the interest yield that the buyer of the CP will obtain. A bigger discount means a larger interest yield for the investor.

The interest yield that the company issuing CP must pay will depend on the credit rating given to its CP program. Suppose that at the start of a CP program, the company can issue three-month paper at a price of $98 ($98 per $100 face value of paper). If three-month interest rates were to rise, and given no change in the credit rating of the CP program, the company might be able to issue new three-month paper only at a lower price of, perhaps, $97. However, if the credit rating of the program were to fall as well, the price at which three-month paper could be issued would be even lower, for example $96, and its cost of borrowing would be higher.

Other Types of Interest-Rate Exposure

In addition to the risk from a change in the general level of interest rates, three other types of interest rate exposure can be identified.

Exposure	Nature of the Risk
Fixed-rate or floating-rate interest	There is a risk of higher interest charges by borrowing on a fixed basis when a floating-rate basis would have been cheaper; or borrowing on a floating-rate basis when a fixed rate would have been cheaper.
Term of funding: the yield curve	There is a risk that a change in the yield curve will make it more expensive to have borrowed short-term rather than long-term; or long-term rather than short-term.
Currency of funding	There is a risk that borrowing in one currency will be more expensive than borrowing in a different currency. Interest-rate risk and foreign-currency risk are both involved because movements in the exchange rate for currency during the term of the loan will add to or reduce the overall cost of borrowing in that currency by increasing the value of the loan in the borrower's domestic currency.

Interest-Rate Exposures and the Balance Sheet

It might help to think of interest-rate exposures in fairly simple terms, by looking at the balance sheet of an organization. Most non-bank organizations have most of their interest-rate exposures on just one side of their balance sheet, as assets (e.g. investments) or as liabilities (loans and other interest-bearing debts). In other words, most non-bank organizations have more interest-sensitive liabilities than interest-sensitive assets, or more interest-sensitive assets than interest-sensitive liabilities.

- Trading or manufacturing companies that borrow extensively to finance their operations have interest-rate exposures on the liability side of their balance sheets, from bank facilities, bond issues and so on.
- Investment institutions have large interest-rate exposures on the assets side of their balance sheets, from interest-bearing investments.

Commercial banks have interest-rate-sensitive assets and liabilities in more or less equal amounts. Exposures therefore can arise on either side of their balance sheets. Because most of the instruments traded by banks are interest-rate sensitive, exposure management (risk management) is of crucial importance.

Off-Balance-Sheet Instruments
Looking at a balance sheet does not give a complete insight into the interest-rate exposures of an organization. This is because the organization might have entered financial transactions that do not appear on its balance sheet. These are off-balance-sheet items that might be used as a means of managing interest rate risk, or even as a means of increasing risk. Off-balance-sheet instruments include a range of financial derivative instruments such as FRAs, futures, swaps and options.

However, reporting on interest-rate exposures in company accounts is a fairly complex topic, and outside the scope of this text.

Interest Rates and their Volatility

Interest-rate risk occurs because interest rates change over time and movements are not predictable regarding direction (up or down), amount or timing. Volatility in interest rates refers to the regularity, pattern of movement and size of changes in rates over time. Greater volatility implies greater interest-rate risk.

Why Interest Rates Change

The general level of interest rates in a free-market economy is determined mainly by market forces - supply and demand for funds. There may be government influence or intervention also.

Market demand to borrow funds and the supply of savings and investment funds will be affected by the following factors.

- Economic conditions. Economic growth is likely to increase the demand for finance from companies to pay for new investments, and consumers. In contrast, during a recession, the credit risk of many would-be borrowers worsens, and banks and other investors become more reluctant to lend.
- Expectations about the economy, such as the rate of economic growth and the rate of inflation. Interest rates generally will rise or fall with changes in the expected or actual rate of inflation.
- The size of government borrowing, either short-term or long-term, adding to the demand for funds in the markets. To borrow in large amounts, a government will have to offer high rates of interest, that will have the effect of raising interest rates on other loans in the markets.

- The government's monetary policy. The value of a country's currency in the foreign-exchange markets (its exchange rate) and the interest rates obtainable on investments in that currency are closely linked. High interest rates are needed to persuade investors to keep their funds in a weak currency or to invest more funds in the currency. Interest rates also might be maintained at a high level in order to control the rate of inflation in the economy.

  A government also can use monetary policy to influence interest rates by controlling the volume of credit lending and borrowing, perhaps by placing restrictions on banks. Official credit controls affect interest rates by restricting the demand for lending or borrowing.

Example

In the past, the UK government has used restrictions on hire purchase (consumer credit) sales to control interest rates. This measure was designed to reduce consumer demand for borrowing. Individuals wishing to buy goods on hire purchase were required to make a down payment of a quarter or one-third of the purchase price and could use hire purchase finance only for the balance. A comparable measure could be a tax on credit cards.

Benchmark Rates

There are many different interest rates offered or charged in the financial markets, including bank deposit rates, mortgage rates, overdraft rates, rates of interest on government loan stock and corporate bonds. However, a few key rates of interest are benchmarks against which other interest rates are set. It is useful to be aware of what some of these benchmark interest rates represent.

- LIBOR (sterling and dollar) and euribor
- LIBID
- Fed funds rate

- US prime rate
- government bond rates (such as yields on US Treasury bonds or UK gilt-edged stock).

LIBOR (London Interbank Offered Rate)

LIBOR is the rate at which banks will offer to lend funds in the London interbank money market to other top-quality banks. It is the rate at which a bank will currently lend to a prime bank. A bank will have a different LIBOR rate for loans of differing maturities. For example, it will have a LIBOR rate for overnight lending, a seven-day LIBOR rate, one-month LIBOR rate, two-month LIBOR rate, three-month LIBOR rate, four-month LIBOR rate and so on, up to a lending period of about one year. The most common LIBOR periods are:

- overnight
- one week
- one month
- three months
- six months
- twelve months.

LIBOR varies according to the term of lending so that a LIBOR rate for a one-year loan will be different from the LIBOR rate applicable to overnight borrowing. For example, one-week sterling LIBOR might be quoted at 6.125% while three-month LIBOR might be quoted at 7.00%.

LIBOR rates are the main money market benchmark rates, and they change continually, varying throughout the day, typically in multiples of one thirty-second of one per cent. Every bank makes its own decision about the rate at which it will lend to other banks at any time.

LIBOR can be quoted for almost any currency although sterling and dollar LIBOR are the most common.

Many commercial loans, particularly large loans, are made at a margin above a bank's LIBOR. rate. The rate of interest payable is reset for each subsequent interest period by reference to the LIBOR rate. For example, if a company obtains a five-year loan, with interest payable every six months at 100 basis points (one per cent) above the six-month LIBOR rate, the interest rate for each subsequent interest period will be determined by reference to the current six-month LIBOR rate. LIBOR-linked loans are the norm for medium-term borrowing by medium-sized and large companies.

Floating-rate loans tend to have their interest rate linked to three-month or six-month LIBOR depending on the frequency of the reset or rollover period.

For terms longer than 12 months, rates for fixed-rate loans tend to be linked to the cost of government debt or to the swap rate, rather than LIBOR.

The interbank market is large and active. Banks will quote an interest rate to other banks for large short-term loans, and the rate that it quotes will depend on market conditions at the time and the credit status of the borrowing bank. Even in the banking world, some banks have a higher credit standing than others, and a bank will lend to a prime bank or blue-chip bank, at a lower rate of interest than it will lend to another bank with lower credit standing.

Screen Rates for LIBOR

For reference purposes, and for use with various financial instruments and loans, a benchmark rate for LIBOR is measured by the British Bankers' Association (BBA) that obtains the interbank lending rate for different lending periods from a number of selected banks, at 11 a.m. each day. The rates supplied by these banks are then used to derive an official LIBOR rate (the BBA LIBOR rate).

The BBA LIBOR rate is issued to the market via the screens of financial information providers such as Reuters and Bloomberg. LIBOR rates also are published daily in the financial press.

Screen-based LIBOR rates provide a useful item of reference information for banks and other organizations. They also are used to fix interest rates on some loans such as syndicated loans, and are used as reference for some interest-rate derivative instruments such as interest-rate futures and interest-rate options.

The BBA calculates LIBOR rates daily for sterling by obtaining the current rates being quoted to 16 reference or contributor banks in London, all prime banks, just before 11.00 a.m. These are the rates at which the contributor bank could borrow, were it to do so, by asking for and then accepting inter-bank offers for loans in reasonable market size. The highest four and lowest four of these rates are ignored, and the LIBOR rate is taken as the average of the remaining eight rates.

Non-sterling LIBOR rates
LIBOR is also the main benchmark rate for offshore lending in a number of currencies known as eurocurrency lending. This is because of London's stature as a major international financial centre. There is a large and active market in London for short-term loans and deposits in currencies other than sterling. Screen rates are published by the BBA for non-sterling loans and deposits. For example, there is:

- a dollar LIBOR rate, sometimes referred to as the dollar LIBOR interbank fixing rate
- a euro LIBOR rate, for loans in euros by London banks.

Another screen rate for interbank loans in euros is the euribor rate. This is a composite rate calculated by the European Banking Federation from interbank rates offered by nearly 50 banks within the euro area, rather than just by London banks.

Euribor
Until the advent of the euro, LIBOR rates were used as the benchmark for lending in various European currencies, notably the Deutschemark and the Italian lira. Other European financial centres could compete against LIBOR rates only as lending benchmarks for their domestic currency, and only the French PIBOR rate (Paris Inter Bank Offered Rate) and the Japanese TIBOR rate (Tokyo Inter Bank Offered Rate)

had more status as a benchmark rate than the comparable LIBOR rates for the French franc and the yen.

The situation changed considerably with the advent of the euro. Europe's leading banks gave their support to a new benchmark rate, the euribor rate. This is a rate derived from the lending rates quoted by 57 banks, mainly banks in continental Europe that was launched in January 1999.

Since its launch, the euribor rate has gained greater acceptance as a benchmark rate than the euro LIBOR rate.

Fed funds rate

The Fed funds rate is a key short-term interest rate in the US. It is the rate at which commercial banks can obtain funds in the Federal funds market, and the rate at which the government (the Federal Reserve) will supply funds. All other short-term interest rates in the US money markets relate to the Fed funds rate, and so any changes in this rate will trigger changes in interest rates throughout the US markets.

US Prime Rate

The prime rate is an administered US interest rate, equivalent to base rate in the UK. It is the benchmark rate against which corporate and personal overdraft borrowing is priced. The prime rate tends to be higher than short-term US money-market rates. Term bank loans in dollars are priced against the more competitive dollar LIBOR benchmarks rather than at a margin above prime rate.

Government bond rates

The interest rates on medium-term and long-term bond issues and on fixed-rate loans by banks might be quoted as a margin over the cost of government borrowing in that country. Government debt of the major economies such as the US, Japan, France, Germany, Switzerland and the UK is perceived as risk-free. The margin above the government bond rate for fixed-rate corporate loans and debt issues reflects the greater risk of the company defaulting compared with loans to the government. Corporate borrowers can pay from 20 basis points (0.20 per cent) per annum up to 500 basis points (5.0 per cent) per annum over the government's cost of funds for a similar maturity depending on the company's credit ratings and the term of the loan.

Key government bond benchmarks are:

- US Treasury bonds
- UK gilts
- German Bunds and French government bonds (euro-denominated)
- Japanese government bonds (JGBs).

Short-term, medium-term and long-term interest rates
A distinction is sometimes made between short-term, medium-term and long-term interest rates.

- *Money market rates* are short-term rates, but refer specifically to interest rates on a range of money-market financial instruments with maturities of up to about a year.
- *Short-term* interest rates include money-market rates and also refer to loans and investments of up to two years or so. They include interbank lending rates, Certificate of Deposit rates and Treasury bill rates. (In the UK, the term short-dated in relation to gilts (shorts) means British government stocks with up to five years left to maturity.)
- *Medium-term* interest rates are rates on loans and investments of around two to seven years or so. Many bank loans are medium-term. Medium-term government bonds, however, might be defined as bonds with between five and 15 years remaining to maturity.
- *Long-term* loans and investments often take the form of issued securities such as government bonds, bonds issued by supranational organizations such as the World Bank and some corporate bonds. Long-dated government bonds might be

defined as those with over 15 years to maturity and undated stock (stock that never will be redeemed). Long-term loans include loans tied to a home loan (mortgage) on real estate.

The distinction between short, medium, and long-term interest rates is not clear cut, but it is nevertheless of some importance. Interest rates vary according to the term of the loan or investment for fixed-rate loans and investments, or according to the period of time between fixing dates for variable-rate loans and investments. The pattern of variation in interest rates according to their term or time period is known as the *yield curve* or *term structure* of interest rates.

LIBID (London Interbank Bid Rate)

Banks will bid to attract large short-term deposits from other banks. So long as the rate it pays on deposits is less than the rate at which it can re-lend to other banks, a bank will make a profit on its loans and deposits business in the interbank market. A bank's London Interbank Bid Rate or LIBID is the rate of interest that it will pay a prime bank for deposits. A bank's LIBID rate is usually about one eighth of one per cent below its LIBOR rate.

Fixed and Variable Interest Rates

Loans and investments offer either a fixed or a variable rate of interest over their term to maturity. A fixed-rate loan carries the same nominal percentage interest rate over the full period of the loan. A floating-rate or variable loan involves the interest rate being changed at regular reset or rollover dates during the loan period.

Long-term bank loans are more often variable-rate loans, with rollover dates at quarterly, half-yearly or yearly intervals. Short-term bank loans allow the borrower to have the choice between a fixed or a floating rate. For example, if a company wants to borrow $1 million for one year, it might be given the choice of

- a loan with a rate of interest fixed at 125 basis points (1¼%) over 12-month LIBOR; or
- a floating-rate loan with a rate of interest set at 125 basis points (1¼%) over three-month LIBOR, with quarterly rollover dates. This means the rate will be refixed every three months at 125 basis points (1¼%) over the level of three-month LIBOR at that time; or
- a floating-rate loan with a rate of interest set at 125 basis points (1¼%) over six-month LIBOR, with a rollover date after six months (mid-way through the loan term).

Changes in Interest Rates and Interest-Rate Cycles

There are very many different interest rates, all of them changing, either regularly or occasionally, by different amounts. Occasionally some interest rates might rise as others fall. For example, money market interest rates might fall as long-term interest rates rise.

However, interest rates are related to each other, and if short-term interest rates rise for some financial instruments or loans, it should be expected that other short-term rates also will rise. We can speak therefore of rises or falls in the general level of interest rates, even though some rates might rise or fall by different amounts.

Changes in the general level of interest rates might be up or down. Over time, it is inevitable that rates will follow a pattern of up followed by down, up again, down again and so on. This pattern of movements can be analyzed between

- small short-term variations; and
- long-term trends in the movement.

A long-term trend of up followed by down, or down followed by up, is called an *interest-rate cycle*.

Interest-Rate Cycles

Economists, governments, bankers, financiers and corporate treasurers monitor the interest-rate cycles of benchmark interest rates, and attempt to predict the size and duration of the cycle. The issues to determine are:

- whether the next movement will be up or down
- when an upward trend will be reversed and the interest rate peaks, or when a downward trend will be reversed and interest rates start to climb again.

Does the Interest-Rate Cycle Exist?

An interest-rate cycle is linked to the business cycle in the underlying economy. When the economy is in a recession, interest rates tend to fall. The government might encourage lower rates to stimulate the economy. At the peak of a business cycle, the demand for loans from growing businesses should push up interest rates to a higher level. Business cycles can be seen to exist in retrospect, but the frequency and range of a cycle varies between each peak and trough.

However, because phases of relative economic growth and decline have been observed historically, it is reasonable to suppose that the same general pattern of business cycles will continue in the future.

Analyzing previous business cycles confirms that:

- cycles in short-term interest rates seem to coincide with business cycles, with interest rates higher at business-cycle peaks; and
- cycles in long-term interest rates exist, but are less volatile than short-term rate cycles, and peaks and troughs in long-term rates are less likely to coincide with peaks and troughs in the business cycle.

An illustrative example of interest-rate cycles is shown overleaf.

Interest-Rate Cycles

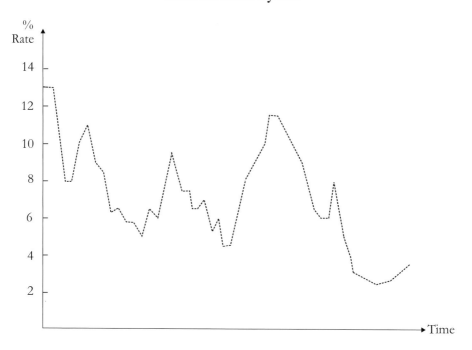

Predicting the Cycle

Predicting when peaks and troughs will occur, or how extreme rate movements might be, is difficult. Judgments about future interest-rate movements therefore are speculative to some extent. Cycles might seem fairly easy to recognize in retrospect, but at any given time it might be difficult to judge what the next movements in interest rates will be. For example, economists might predict that interest rates are nearing the peak of a cycle, and will soon start to fall. However, there may be uncertainty as to just how long it will be before interest rates fall, and until then rates might continue to rise still further.

The Size and Frequency of Interest-Rate Changes

Interest-rate risk is greater when interest rates are volatile. Volatility refers to the size and frequency of changes in rates or prices.

In the table below, there are two rates of interest. Suppose that one is the three-month LIBOR rate for currency X and the other is the three-month LIBOR rate for currency Y.

Time period	Interest rate X	Interest rate Y
1	5%	4.5%
2	5.25%	5%
3	5%	6%
4	4.75%	4%
5	5%	5.5%

Taking a simple arithmetical average for simplicity of illustration, the average rate of interest for both currency X and currency Y over the five periods is the same, 5%. However, interest rates in currency Y have fluctuated by larger amounts, and the interest rate for currency Y has clearly been more volatile than for currency X.

For business managers or investors concerned about interest-rate risk, their interest-related assets or liabilities in currency Y would be considered to carry greater interest-rate risk than those in currency X.

Even in advanced economies interest rates have been known to fluctuate substantially. In the UK for example, three-month sterling LIBOR fluctuated in the late 1980s and early 1990s between a high of about 15.2% and a low of about 5.5%. For a company with variable-rate sterling debts of £10 million, a one-per-cent increase in interest rates will result in additional interest costs of £100,000 per annum. Therefore a company that took out a £10 million variable-rate loan near the end of 1989 at LIBOR plus 1% would have experienced an increase in interest charges from an annual rate from about £1,600,000 (16%) to about £650,000 million (6.5%) by the end of 1993.

Changes in the general level of interest rates over the period of a loan or investment can be expected to be broadly in line with changes in the rate of inflation, and in the state of the economy.

Money-market rates also respond directly to supply and demand in the market. Just a small change in the rate can be important to a borrower or lender. For example, on a $20 million three-month loan, each change of 0.01% p.a. in the rate would be worth $500 ($20 million x 0.01% x 3/12). For a larger company with variable-rate debts of $1 billion, an increase of just one basis point in the interest rate (0.01 per cent) would mean additional interest costs of $100,000 per annum.

Variations up or down can be very small, but a borrower would still hope to arrange a loan when the rate is lower and a lender when the rate is higher. Timing a transaction can be worth several thousand dollars in extra cost or lower revenue.

Measuring Volatility
The volatility of an interest rate, such as three-month dollar LIBOR, can be measured statistically. Historical volatility is a measure of variations in the interest rate over a selected period of time in the past. If it can be assumed that volatility will remain roughly the same in the future, historical volatility can provide a guide to future volatility in the interest rate.

This text does not go into the mathematical detail of computing volatility. However, in general terms historical data is obtained by taking the interest rate at a selected regular interval over a given period of time. For example:

- we can measure ten-day volatility in the three-month dollar LIBOR rate by taking the current dollar LIBOR rate at ten-day intervals over a period of five years
- similarly we can measure 30-day volatility in the three-month dollar LIBOR rate by taking the current dollar LIBOR rate at 30-day intervals over the same period.

Volatility varies according to the time interval selected. Choosing the time period depends on the intended use of the volatility measurement. Ten-day volatility can be used to predict the future movement in the interest rate over the next ten-day period, and 30-day volatility can be used to predict the future movement in the interest rate over the next 30-day period.

The selected data, for example, values of 30-day volatility for the three-month dollar LIBOR rate over a five-year period, are then used to measure price relatives, the proportional change in the interest rate from one period to the next. For example, if the rate goes up from 8% to 8.5% from one period to the next, there has been a rate change by a factor of 1.0625 (8.5/8.0). The price relative therefore is 1.0625. Similarly, if the rate falls from 7% in one period to 6.75% in the next, the rate change is by a factor of 0.96429 (6.75/7.0) and the price relative therefore is 0.96429.

It is assumed that changes in interest rates from one period to the next, as measured by price relatives, are log-normally distributed. A standard deviation of interest-rate changes then can be measured from the data for price relatives. This is a statistical measurement of volatility in the interest rate over the selected period in the past that can be used for predictive purposes.

Information services such as Bloomberg provide measurements of volatility for a variety of time intervals; the user of the service simply can select the particular measurement required.

Interest-rate volatility is used in various ways. For example, it is used in the pricing of interest-rate options.

The Usefulness of Volatility
Given a statistical assumption of a normal distribution, measurements of volatility and the standard deviation in volatility might be used to predict the probable extent of interest-rate changes to the end of the next time period. As a rough guide, it can be assumed that over one time

period, the interest rate is unlikely to move up or down by more than twice the volatility.

For example, if 60-day volatility in the three-month dollar LIBOR rate is measured as 20 basis points, and the LIBOR rate for the 60-day period just ended is 7%, it might be predicted that the three-month LIBOR rate in 60 days' time is unlikely to be above 7.40% (7% + (2 x 0.20%)) or below 6.60% (7% - (2 x 0.20%)).

For banks, volatility measurements can be used to manage their exposures to a rise or fall in a particular interest rate. For example, suppose that a bank has an exposure for the next ten days to a rise in six-month dollar LIBOR. For each basis point rise (0.01%) in the six-month LIBOR rate, the bank might lose, for example, $50,000. If ten-day volatility in the six-month dollar LIBOR rate is 12 basis points, the bank could estimate its maximum likely loss from its exposure to be $1.2 million (2 x 12 x $50,000).

Volatility also can be used to set a limit on the interest-rate exposure a bank is prepared to tolerate. For example, suppose that a bank wishes to take a position in interest-rate instruments, for example by writing interest-rate options. This will create an exposure to a rise or fall in a particular interest rate, for example three-month sterling LIBOR over the next 30 days. The bank can look at 30-day volatility in three-month sterling LIBOR and assess the maximum probable rise or fall in the interest rate over the next 30-day period. If the bank sets a limit to the maximum loss it is willing to take on its options positions, it can decide the maximum amount of interest-rate options it is prepared to write.

Summary

While future interest-rate changes cannot be predicted with accuracy as to direction, timing and size of movement, they are significant for:

- the cost of borrowing or income from investments
- deciding *when* to borrow or invest

- deciding *for how long* to borrow or invest
- choosing a currency of borrowing or investment
- selecting the instrument or method for borrowing or lending.

Volatility can be measured statistically, however, in order to carry out a probability analysis of the possible size of interest-rate movements in the future. Banks and other financial institutions also can use measurements of volatility to set limits to their risk from exposures to interest-rate changes.

4

Fixed or Floating-Rate Interest

Organizations should try to contain interest-rate risk on borrowing, lending and investing by seeking a suitable balance between fixed and variable-rate instruments.

Risks for the Borrower

Borrowing can be at a fixed rate of interest for the full term of a loan, although banks prefer not to lend at fixed rates beyond about five years. Large companies can borrow long term at a fixed rate by issuing corporate bonds. Alternatively, borrowing can be at a variable or floating rate, where the interest rate is reset periodically in line with the current market rate.

There can be a risk in choosing the more expensive borrowing option, fixed or floating rate. For example, a fixed rate of 8% would have been better than a variable rate, initially at 8%, if interest rates rose during the period of the loan. Conversely, it is better to borrow at a variable rate than at a fixed rate when interest rates are falling, in order to benefit from the progressively lower cost of funds.

Because the risk is two-way, risk is unavoidable for every borrower. Borrowing at a fixed rate creates an exposure to falling interest rates, and borrowing at a variable rate creates an exposure to rising interest rates.

The advantage of corporate borrowing at a fixed rate is that the cost of financing is known and certain. An organization can use the cost of borrowing to assess the financial viability of any project or investment for which it intends to use the money it has borrowed. The project might be undertaken if the returns it is expected to generate exceed the known cost of the borrowing to finance it.

On the other hand, a company will not want to lock itself into a fixed rate for long-term borrowing if there is a risk that interest rates might fall substantially. High financing costs would put it at a disadvantage against competitor organizations.

Borrowing at Fixed or Floating Rate

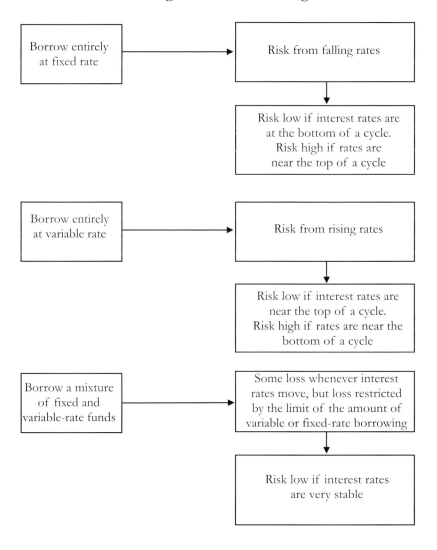

The risk of choosing the wrong type of borrowing, fixed or floating, will be reduced if it can be anticipated which way interest rates will move over the term of the loan. However, this is not always easy.

It is sometimes possible to forecast future interest-rate changes when they are progressively moving up or down. For example, when short-term interest rates are very high and the economy is threatened with recession, it would be reasonable to forecast that the next movements in interest rates will be down. It is, however, hard to predict when the top or bottom of a cycle will be reached or the timing and pace of any change in interest rates. So while companies might be certain that interest rates will be significantly lower or higher during the next one, two or three years, they will be far less certain *when* interest rates might fall or rise.

This aspect makes some risk unavoidable for indebted or cash-rich companies, even after predicting future trends, and management should try to minimize or contain the risk.

Example 1
Suppose that between October Year 1 and October Year 2, UK base rates are 10%, at their highest level for many years. In April Year 2, a medium-sized company seeking a two-year loan of £2,000,000 has been offered finance by its bank at either a fixed rate of 12%, or at a variable rate with the three-monthly rollover periods at LIBOR plus 3%. LIBOR currently is 10.3%.

Most companies believe that sterling interest rates will not rise any further. But for a company seeking a two-year loan, the problem would be to decide when interest rates might start to fall, by how much and *how quickly*.

Analysis
Borrowing at LIBOR (13.3%) initially would be more expensive by 1.3%, and an early fall in rates would be required for variable-rate borrowing to be cheaper.

Suppose that as events turn out, three-month LIBOR at the reset dates for the loan would have been approximately

Reset date	3-month LIBOR	Loan rate (LIBOR + 3%)
Start of loan, April Year 2	10.3%	13.3%
July Year 2	9.9%	12.9%
October Year 2	9.5%	12.5%
January Year 3	8.7%	11.7%
April Year 3	6.9%	9.9%
July Year 3	6.1%	9.1%
October Year 3	5.4%	8.4%
January Year 4	5.7%	8.7%

The average annual rate for the variable rate loan would have been less than 11% that would have been less than a fixed rate loan at 12%. However, the cost of variable-rate interest would not have fallen below the fixed rate of 12% until the third interest period, from January Year 3. In this case, the variable-rate loan option would have cost about £40,000 less over a two-year period.

In this example, there was a reasonable expectation when the loan was arranged that interest rates had peaked and were about to fall, and the variable-rate loan option was probably the least-risk choice. If interest rates had remained high, however, and three-month LIBOR had not fallen below 9%, the fixed-rate loan option would have been cheaper. By selecting a variable-rate loan, the company took on an exposure to interest rates remaining high. An essential point to recognize, therefore, is that for a borrower, exposure to the risk of having chosen the more expensive option, fixed or floating rate, is unavoidable.

Example 2

Towards the end of Year 1, a large US company was planning its funding requirements from the middle of Year 2 and decides that it wants to raise $50 million. Two options under consideration are a variable-rate loan and a five-year fixed-rate loan, for which the interest rate would be fixed at a margin above the current yield on five-year Treasuries. The current five-year Treasuries yield is 6.5%, having been as low as 5.75% in May of the previous year. However, the US economy is showing signs of overheating and the rate of inflation is rising.

Analysis

The company has two problems. The first is selecting between a variable-rate loan and a fixed-rate loan. In this situation, the rising rate of inflation might suggest that interest rates also will rise, although it would be uncertain for how long. This might persuade the company to prefer fixed-rate borrowing to variable-rate borrowing. However, a five-year term for a fixed-rate loan is quite long, and the company would have to consider the likely movements in short-term rates over the five-year borrowing period. A second problem, having selected fixed-rate borrowing, would be *when* to borrow. The funds are required at some time in the middle of next year. If interest rates are expected to rise, there would be a case for borrowing the money early to secure a lower rate of interest, and keep the funds on deposit until required.

It could be argued that large companies should plan their funding over the long term, and that fixed-rate borrowing should be undertaken whenever an opportunity seems suitable, at the cyclical low in the market.

Using interest-rate swaps to manage the balance between fixed and floating-rate debt

The problem in choosing between fixed-rate and variable-rate borrowing is eased to some extent by the availability of *interest-rate swaps*. These allow a company to switch from fixed-rate borrowing to floating-rate borrowing, or from floating-rate borrowing to fixed-rate borrowing.

For example, suppose a company borrows $40 million at a variable rate of interest, but interest rates start to rise and seem likely to carry on rising. If the company decides that it would like to switch to borrowing at a fixed rate, it can negotiate a swap agreement with a specialist bank, and start paying at a fixed rate rather than a variable rate. However, given that interest rates already have started to rise, the cost of its fixed-rate borrowing with the swap will be higher than if the company had negotiated a fixed-rate loan from the outset.

Similarly, suppose that a company borrows $60 million at a 7% fixed rate of interest, but interest rates start to fall and are expected to continue falling. It could arrange to switch from fixed rate interest costs to variable-rate costs by arranging an interest-rate swap. However, if interest rates already have started to fall by the time the swap is arranged, the company will incur higher interest costs by choosing initially to borrow at a variable rate.

The details of interest-rate (coupon) swap arrangements are not explained in this text. The point to note is that swaps can be used to manage the balance between fixed and floating-rate borrowing, but there is nevertheless an unavoidable risk in the initial choice between fixed rate or floating-rate borrowing.

Risk for the Lender

The risk for the lender should be the mirror image of the risk for the borrower. To maximize profits a bank should prefer to lend at a fixed rate when it expects interest rates to fall, and at a variable rate when rates are expected to rise.

In general, however, commercial banks do not speculate excessively on future interest-rate movements. They usually hedge their interest-rate exposures by matching their fixed-rate lending with fixed-rate funds, and their variable-rate lending with variable-rate funds. Interest-rate swaps can help them to manage this matching.

Because most commercial bank lending is financed by variable-rate funds (customer deposits and money-market loans), a bank has a large degree of protection. So long as banks can relend at a variable rate higher than the cost of their variable-rate fund, and the credit risk from bad debts on loans is negligible, there should be a secure profit from the spread.

Banks may take on some risk with rollover finance. However, they will keep the risk within acceptable limits. For example, a bank might borrow six-month funds on the interbank market and relend the money as a variable-rate loan with three-monthly rollover dates, at a margin above LIBOR. The risk for the bank would be that the three-month LIBOR rate might fall before the first rollover date for the loan, thereby reducing its interest income from the loan. In the second three-month period, the income from the loan might be even less than the comparable cost of the interest on the six-month borrowing.

Fixed-rate lending by banks might be restricted, to avoid exposure to a rise in interest rates. Banks rarely will offer fixed-rate loans beyond five years and might not lend at a fixed rate beyond one or two years to some customers. In this way, banks can contain the risk when they are financed primarily by variable-rate funds. However, as mentioned earlier, fixed-rate lending is less risky, and so has become more common following the availability of interest-rate swaps. Banks can use a swap to lock in a fixed cost of borrowing, and can lend to customers at a higher fixed rate, thus securing a profit.

Risk for the Investor

An investor in interest-bearing deposits and securities could choose to place funds in short-term or variable-rate deposits, and earn interest linked to a current market yield. Alternatively, the investor could choose fixed-rate investments, typically long-term marketable securities such as government bonds or eurobonds. There is also choice in the timing and duration of investments. Because many fixed rate securities are freely traded in the markets, an investor can switch at will from fixed to variable-rate investments and back again.

Companies that are cash-rich can opt to invest in floating-rate instruments that should ensure the market value of their portfolio remains fairly constant, regardless of rises or falls in interest rates. For example, suppose that an interest-bearing investment yielding 15 basis points below LIBOR has a market value of 100. If interest rates rise, the yield on the investment will rise also at the next rollover or reset date for interest, and the value of the investment should remain at or around 100. A drawback to investing in floating rate or short-term investments, however, is that yields could be much higher on fixed-rate investments over a longer term to maturity.

Variable-rate investments will earn more income than fixed-rate investments when interest rates are rising. For example, if the current yield on ten-year gilts is 7%, and variable rate deposits yield 6.5%, the fixed-rate option would be more profitable. However, if interest rates were to rise, the yield on the variable-rate deposits would go up, but the gilts would continue to pay a fixed income to the bondholder.

When interest rates rise, the market value of fixed-rate investments will fall. For example, suppose that the yield on 20-year government bonds is 10%. Bonds paying a coupon rate of 8% would have a market value of about $80 per $100 nominal value. (This is calculated as the par value of $100 multiplied by 8/10, a reasonably accurate approximation for long-term bonds.) If the interest-rate yield expected by market investors on government bonds went up to 12%, the market value of these 8% bonds would fall to about $67 per $100 nominal value ($100 x 8/12). A fixed-rate investor who paid $80 when market yields were 10% would therefore see $13 knocked off the value of the investment if market yields rose to 12%.

When market rates of interest fall, the price of fixed-rate investments will rise. Using the same example, if market yields fell to 6%, the price of 20-year 8% government bonds would rise to $133 per $100 nominal value.

Containing the Risk

Although the risk from unfavorable rate movements is unavoidable for the choice between fixed or floating-rate borrowing and investment, companies should seek to keep it under control when borrowing or investing large amounts. It could be argued that companies should develop a clear strategy for the mix of fixed and floating rate instruments in their debt profile or their investment portfolio profile.

The two key concerns therefore should be to:

- establish a balanced mix between fixed and floating-rate funds or investments, and
- try to forecast future movements in interest rates and to time fixed-rate borrowings or fixed and variable-rate investments accordingly.

Some companies can borrow readily at a variable rate but less easily at a fixed rate. Such companies can try to achieve a balance between fixed and floating-rate borrowing, or to limit the risk from adverse changes in the variable rate of interest through risk-management products such as forward-rate agreements, futures, options and swaps.

Overdraft Facility or Short-Term Loan?

A further aspect of interest-rate risk can arise for non-bank corporates in the choice between an overdraft facility and a short-term loan. For a short-term loan, the interest rate might be fixed for the full term of the loan, or reset at rollover dates within the loan period, and charged on the full amount borrowed. Interest on an overdraft is charged at a daily rate but only on the amount by which the borrower is overdrawn.

A bank normally will charge more for arranging an overdraft than for a term loan. In addition to a higher arrangement fee, banks set a higher margin above base rate for an overdraft.

Example
A small UK company believes that it will have to borrow up to £100,000 in the next 12 months. It could arrange an overdraft facility for up to £100,000 at base rate plus 3%, with an arrangement fee of 2%. Alternatively, it could borrow £100,000 at base rate plus 150 basis points

(1.50%) with an arrangement fee of 1%. The company expects that if it chose to borrow on overdraft, the average overdrawn balance would be £60,000. Base rate is 6%.

Analysis

Ignoring interest-rate risk, the overdraft option is cheaper because interest is payable only when the account is overdrawn. If it is assumed that there are no changes in interest rates over the year, an overdraft would cost £7,400 (an arrangement fee of £2,000 plus interest at 9% on an average overdraft balance of £60,000). The one-year loan would cost £8,500 (an arrangement fee of £1,000 plus interest at 7.5% on £100,000).

The overdraft would cost more if interest rates went up during the year, but in this example, interest costs on the average overdraft balance of £60,000 would have to be more than £1,000 higher (£8,500 - £7,400) for the term loan to be cheaper. This would imply an increase in the average interest over the loan period of more than 1.8% (1,100 ÷ 60,000 x 100%) from its level at the start of the year. This would call for an increase in the average base rate from 6% to nearly 8%.

There is an extra interest *cost* risk in choosing an overdraft, however. If the average overdraft balance is higher than expected, interest charges also would be higher. For example, if the average overdraft balance is £80,000 rather than £60,000, the cost of the overdraft, assuming no change in the base rate, would be £9,200 (arrangement fee of £2,000 plus 9% of £80,000), that would be slightly higher than for the one-year loan.

Apart from cost, the main disadvantage of an overdraft facility is that unless the facility is committed, the bank is under no obligation to continue providing the facility. It can withdraw the facility if the company's financial position deteriorates. In contrast, with a fixed-term loan, the bank cannot demand repayment of the loan before the due date so long as the borrower is not in default with the payments.

In general, non-bank corporates tend to prefer overdrafts to short-term loans unless:

- the full overdraft facility will be used up for much of the loan period, or
- interest rates are expected to rise by a large amount during the loan period.

5

Term of Funding.
The Yield Curve

Interest rates exist for loans and deposits for any duration of transaction. It is possible to borrow or invest funds for maturities ranging from one day (overnight) to 25 or 30 years. Some borrowers might be able to obtain a perpetual loan that never requires repayment. Companies will pay more for loans than they will earn on deposits, but the term structure of interest rates is similar for deposits and loans.

Yield Curve

The term structure of interest rates, or yield curve, shows how selected interest rates, for example selected benchmark rates of interest, vary according to the interest period or period of the loan.

A yield curve can be drawn for a wide variety of financial instruments. The most widely analyzed yield curves are those for benchmark instruments, such as:

- short-term interbank loans between prime quality banks (LIBOR rates, for maturities up to about one year)
- government bond rates, for long-term rates. Benchmark bond issues are taken, one for each chosen maturity, and the current interest yield on these bonds provides the rate for the yield curve. For example, a long-term yield curve can be constructed by selecting a number of government bond issues, with remaining terms to maturity of one year, two years, three, four, five, seven, ten, 15, 20 and 30 years. The yield on each issue can be plotted on a graph and the points joined up to produce a

yield curve up to 30 years out. Alternatively, the current yields on all government bond issues can be analyzed, to produce a weighted average yield curve for all maturities.

The reason for selecting interbank rates and government bond rates is to obtain interest rates that can be considered risk-free. The interest rates on these loans or bonds will not be affected by credit-risk issues.

Yield curves also can be:

- historical, i.e. based on current rates in the market, and
- forward-looking. Market estimates of what yields will be in the future can be calculated from current market rates. This is explained in the next chapter.

Information providers such as Bloomberg and Reuters analyze yield curves in a variety of ways. An example of an historical yield curve is shown below.

Slope of the Yield Curve
The normal yield curve is upward-sloping (sometimes referred to as a classical or positive curve). This means that interest rates normally are higher for long-term loans than for short-term loans, to compensate the lender for tying up funds for a long time and the increased credit risk in a long loan. The curve often will flatten out for very long-term loans (15 to 25 years and beyond).

Example
Interest rates on the dollar might be monitored according to yields on Treasury bills and government bonds (Treasuries). The hypothetical data shown overleaf for US interest yields shows an upward-sloping yield curve, as illustrated in the graph on page 57. In this example, the graph starts at a maturity of three months and goes up to a 30-year term.

Dollar Interest Rates

Term	Rate %
3 months	5.940
6 months	6.430
1 year	6.770
2 years	7.450
3 years	7.740
4 years	7.950
5 years	8.060
6 years	8.168
7 years	8.190
8 years	8.219
9 years	8.275
10 years	8.296
15 years	8.403
20 years	8.558
30 years	8.678

Positive Yield Curve

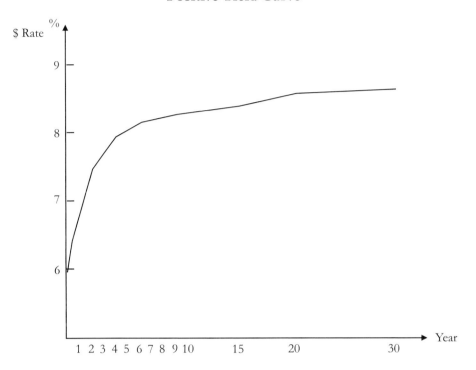

Sometimes the yield curve will be inverse or downward-sloping. This occurs when interest rates are higher on short-term loans than on long-term loans. Inverse yield curves can occur when the inflation rate is high and expected to fall, and interest rates are expected to fall eventually.

Example
An example of an inverse yield curve is shown overleaf. Again, the figures are illustrative only.

Sterling Interest Rates

Term	Rate %
3 months	10.56
6 months	10.69
1 year	10.69
2 years	10.10
3 years	9.99
4 years	9.88
5 years	9.81
6 years	9.70
7 years	9.66
8 years	9.39
9 years	9.40
10 years	9.30
15 years	8.93
20 years	8.86
30 years	8.80

Here, the yield curve rises between three months and six months, and is flat between six months and one year, but is inverse (downward-sloping) beyond one year. This yield curve is shown opposite.

When the yield curve is inverse, the market expects a fall in interest rates at some time in the future.

Inverse Yield Curve: Sterling

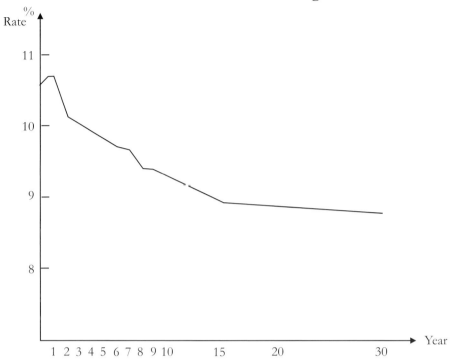

Yield curves do not necessarily follow a continuously upward-sloping or inverse trend.

Yield curves can be flat over a range of maturities. A yield curve also can rise between some maturities and fall between others.

Interest rates change continually, and the yield curve can change shape and direction. For example, if a country with a high rate of inflation begins to bring inflation under control, the yield curve might change from negative (inverse) to positive (upward sloping).

Volatility and the Yield Curve
Changes in the slope of the yield curve can be significant within a relatively short period of time. When the yield curve changes its shape, it follows that interest rates also are volatile.

Risk and the Yield Curve

The risk of changes in the yield curve is one of the interest-rate risks to which a borrower, lender or investor might be exposed, depending on the maturity mix of its borrowed funds or investment or loan portfolio.

By choosing a term for borrowing there is a risk that, in retrospect, an alternative choice of maturities would have been cheaper.

Example

A company wishes to borrow $10 million for three years and is considering two options.

- A variable-rate loan with a rollover every 12 months. The interest rate for the first 12 months would be 7.5%.
- A variable-rate loan with a rollover every six months. The interest rate for the first six months would be 7.75%. (The yield curve is inverse.)

During the three-year term of the loan, the yield curve changes from inverse to positive. Rates are:

After:	6-month rate	12-month rate
6 months	7.25%	Not applicable
1 year	7.25%	7.5%
1½ years	7.25%	Not applicable
2 years	6.25%	6.5%
2 ½ years	6.25%	Not applicable

Interest costs over the three-year period would be:

Alternative 1: 12-month rollover	$
2 x 7.5% x $10 million	1,500,000
+1 x 6.5% x $10 million	650,000
Total interest cost	2,150,000

Alternative 2: 6-month rollover	$
6/12 x 7.75% x $10 million	387,500
+ 3 x 6/12 x 7.25% x $10 million	1,087,500
+ 2 x 6/12 x 6.25% x $10 million	625,000
Total interest cost	2,100,000

In retrospect, the six-months rollover option would have been $50,000 cheaper because of the change of direction in the yield curve.

For large companies that borrow heavily, choosing the best borrowing term could make a difference of several hundred thousand dollars in interest.

Exercise

A company wishing to borrow $20 million for two years at a variable rate of interest has chosen to borrow at three-month LIBOR plus 1% rather than at six-month LIBOR plus 1%. When it made the decision, three-month LIBOR was 6.5% and six-month LIBOR was 6.75%.

Over the period of the loan, interest rates were:

Month	Year	Three-month LIBOR	Six-month LIBOR
3	1	6.25%	6.5%
6	1	5.5%	5.75%
9	1	5.75%	5.75%
12	1	6.5%	6.0%
3	2	7.0%	6.5%
6	2	7.5%	7.0%
9	2	8.0%	7.5%
12	2	7.75%	7.5%

The change in the yield curve at the end of Year 1 followed a rise in the rate of inflation.

Did the company select the lower-cost borrowing option? What was the cost difference?

Solution

With three-month rollover dates, and interest at LIBOR plus 1%, interest costs would have been as follows:

Period	LIBOR	Interest rate on loan	Approximate interest cost	$000
Months 1-3, Year 1	6.5%	7.5%	(3/12 x $20 million x 7.5%)	375.0
Months 4-6, Year 1	6.25%	7.25%	(3/12 x $20 million x 7.25%)	362.5
Months 7-9, Year 1	5.5%	6.5%	(3/12 x $20 million x 6.5%)	325.0
Months 10-12, Year 1	5.75%	6.75%	(3/12 x $20 million x 6.75%)	337.5
Months 1-3, Year 2	6.5%	7.5%	(3/12 x $20 million x 7.5%)	375.0
Months 4-6, Year 2	7.0%	8.0%	(3/12 x $20 million x 8.0%)	400.0
Months 7-9, Year 2	7.5%	8.5%	(3/12 x $20 million x 8.5%)	425.0
Months 10-12, Year 2	8.0%	9.0%	(3/12 x $20 million x 9.0%)	450.0
Total interest charge				3,050.0

When six-monthly rollover dates were incorporated, interest charges would have been:

Period	LIBOR	Interest rate on loan	Approximate interest cost	$000
Months 1-6, Year 1	6.75%	7.75%	(6/12 x $20 million x 7.75%)	775.0
Months 7-12, Year 1	5.75%	6.75%	(6/12 x $20 million x 6.75%)	675.0
Months 1-6, Year 2	6.0%	7.0%	(6/12 x $20 million x 7.0%)	700.0
Months 7-12, Year 2	7.0%	8.0%	(6/12 x $20 million x 8.0%)	800.0
Total interest charge				2,950.0

In retrospect the company chose the higher-cost option, paying $100,000 more in interest costs than if it had chosen the six-monthly rollover-date option.

Risks for Investors

A similar risk faces investors. A change in the yield curve can alter the relative profitability of similar investments with different terms.

Example
An investment company has $100 million to invest for one year in short-term money-market investments. The choice is between three-month and six-month Certificates of Deposit (CDs) and the company opts for six-month CDs. The current yield is 5.75% per annum on three-month CDs and 6.25% on six-month CDs. Available rates during the subsequent year were:

After	Three-month CDs	Six-month CDs
3 months	6.25%	6.25%
6 months	6.25%	6.0%
9 months	6.0%	5.75%

Analysis

In retrospect, the company selected a lower-earning investment, despite the change in relative yields from three-month and six-month CDs. A series of four investments in three-month CDs would have earned:

	Interest earned
	$000
Months 1-3 (3/12 x 5.75% x $100 million)	1,437.50
Months 4-6 and 7-9 (3/12 x 6.25% x $100 million)	3,125.00
Months 10-12 (3/12 x 6.0% x $100 million)	1,500.00
Total income	6,062.50

A series of two investments in six-month CDs would have earned:

	Interest earned
	$000
Months 1-6 (6/12 x 6.25% x $100 million)	3,125.00
Months 7-12 (6/12 x 6.0% x $100 million)	3,000.00
	6,125.00

The choice of investing in six-month CDs yielded extra income of $62,500 in the year.

Risks for Lenders

Commercial banks lending short-term or at floating rates of interest obtain most of their funds from short-term sources (customer deposits, interbank loans). Short-term funding and lending decisions can create interest-rate exposures. Banks might be at risk to changes in both the general level of interest rates and the shape of the yield curve. For example, suppose that a bank borrows for three months to finance a six-month loan to a customer, with the intention of borrowing for a further three months at the end of month 3, to renew the funding of the six-month loan. If it does this, the bank will have an exposure during months 1 to 3 to a rise in the three-month borrowing rate. If it has to renew the funding at a higher cost, the net profit from the six-month loan, after deducting the cost of the financing, will be lower.

Limiting the Risk

Exposure to the risk of selecting a more costly borrowing term or a less profitable investment term is unavoidable, in the same way that choosing between fixed or floating rates of interest creates an unavoidable risk. For companies that borrow heavily, the risk can be limited by arranging a mix of loans with differing rollover dates, and investment companies can build up a portfolio of interest-earning investments with differing maturities.

Changes in the yield curve normally are difficult to predict accurately. However, a company could speculate on future changes by switching a greater proportion of its loans or investments from short-term to long-term or long-term to short-term, according to the predicted direction of the change.

Banks can try to control their risks on short-term lending by *analyzing the yield curve* to obtain forward/forward rates. These show the market's predictions about how interest rates will change in the future. Forward/forward rates are fundamental to the workings of the money markets and derivative instruments, for example to forward-rate agreements (FRAs) and short-term interest-rate futures. Forward/forward rates are explained in the next chapter.

6

Forward/Forward Rates and the Yield Curve

In the previous chapter it was explained that the yield curve can be volatile, and it is impossible to predict with certainty how the general level of interest rates or the shape of the yield curve will change in the future.

However, current market interest rates can be used to establish what the markets think interest rates and the yield curve will be in the future. This is done by analyzing the current market yield curve to derive *forward/forward rates* and a *forward yield curve*.

What is a Forward/Forward Rate?

A forward/forward rate also called simply a forward rate, is an interest rate for a loan or deposit period starting at some time in the future, calculated from current interest rates in the market. A forward/forward rate for a loan period with a term of n months, starting at the end of month x, can be obtained from two current interest rates, for terms of x months and (x + n) months. An example of a forward/forward rate is the six-month LIBOR rate starting at the end of month 4, for a period lasting from the end of month 4 to the end of month 10. A measurement of this forward/forward rate can be derived from two current interest rates, the current 4-month and 10-month LIBOR rates.

A forward/forward rate for a term of n months, starting at the end of month x, is the rate of interest at which a bank would have to re-lend in order to break even, if it were to borrow money for (x + n) months and re-lend it for just x months, with the intention of re-lending it at the end of month x for a further n months.

For example, if a bank were to borrow for 10 months at the ten-month LIBOR rate, and initially re-lend the money for four months at the four-month LIBOR rate, the forward/forward rate from the end of month 4 to the end of month 10 is the minimum rate of interest the bank would need just to break even, when it re-lends the money at the end of month 4 for a further 6 months, to the end of month 10.

A *forward yield curve* is a yield curve derived from a number of forward/forward rates. For example, a forward yield curve starting in one month's time can be obtained from current market interest rates (spot rates) for terms of:

- one month and two months, that would be used to derive the one-month forward rate, starting in one month's time
- one month and three months, that would be used to derive the two-month forward rate, starting in one month's time
- one month and four months, that would be used to derive the three-month forward rate, starting in one month's time
- one month and five months, and so on.

A forward yield curve can be used by a bank in various ways. For example, it can be used to price interest-rate derivative instruments such as forward rate agreements (FRAs).

How is a Forward/Forward Rate Calculated?

All the examples in this chapter will be related to short-term (money-market) interest rates. The same principles apply to long-term interest rates, where forward/forward rates can be implied from current interest yields on bonds. The arithmetic for long-term forward rates, however, is more complex, and so is not illustrated here.

The method of calculating a forward/forward money market rate will be explained with an example. Suppose that interest rates are:

Term	Days	Interest rate (per annum)
3 months	92	5.25%
6 months	184	5.50%

The current three-month rate of interest is 5.25%. We do not know what the three-month rate will be three months from now. However, we can calculate what the market expects the three-month rate to be in three months' time simply by comparing the current (spot) three-month rate and six-month rate.

Suppose that a bank lends $1,000 for three months at 5.25% and $1,000 for six months at 5.50%. Interest is calculated for dollars in the money markets on an actual/360-days basis, and this basis is used in the calculations that follow. The bank's returns from its three-month and six-month loans will be as follows:

Time Diagram

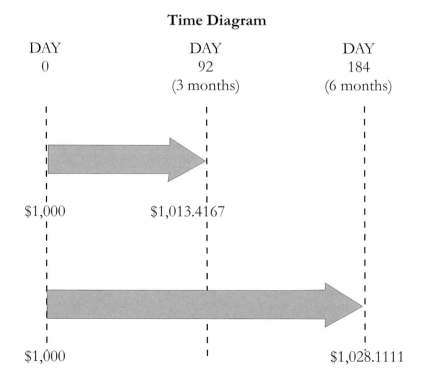

DAY 0	DAY 92 (3 months)	DAY 184 (6 months)
$1,000	$1,013.4167	
$1,000		$1,028.1111

Workings

3 months $1,000 x $\left[1 + \left(\dfrac{5.25}{100} \; x \; \dfrac{92}{360}\right)\right]$ = $1,013.4167

6 months $1,000 x $\left[1 + \left(\dfrac{5.5}{100} \; x \; \dfrac{184}{360}\right)\right]$ = $1,028.1111

To the bank, lending for three months to earn $1,013.4167 and lending
for six months to earn $1,028.1111 have the same current value (present
value) of $1,000 because the bank is indifferent between earning
$1,013.4167 after three months and $1,028.1111 after six months.
Therefore it can be argued that the bank would expect, if it lent for three
months, to be able to re-lend $1,013.4167 after three months and be able
to earn $1,028.1111 by the end of month 6.

Time Diagram

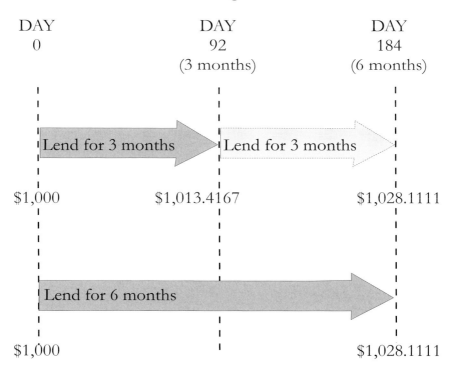

The implied three-month interest rate for the second three-month period, from the end of month 3 to the end of month 6, is calculated as follows:

Step 1
Calculate the interest earned.

	$
End value	1,028.1111
Initial loan	1,013.4167
Interest earned	14.6944

Step 2
A formula for calculating the interest rate is:

$$R \quad = \quad \frac{I}{P} \quad \times \quad \frac{360}{D}$$

Where:

- R is the interest rate (as an annual rate)
- I is the interest earned in the forward period
- P is the amount of the loan (or deposit) at the start of the forward period
- D is the number of calendar days in the loan or deposit period.

  (365 days rather than 360 days would be used to calculate forward/forward rates for a number of currencies, notably sterling, for which money-market interest is calculated on an actual/365 basis.)

In this example, the implied three-month forward/forward rate from the end of month 3 to the end of month 6 is:

$$R \quad = \quad \frac{\$14.6944}{\$1,013.4167} \quad \times \quad \frac{360}{(184 - 92)} \quad = 5.674\% \text{ per annum}$$

Further Example
Suppose current interest rates in the sterling money markets are as
follows:

Term	Days	Interest rate (per annum)
3 months	92	6.0%
6 months	181	6.5%
9 months	273	7.0%
12 months	365	7.25%

What six-month forward/forward rates can be implied from these spot
rates for:

- months 4 to 9 (end of month 3 to end of month 9)
- months 7 to 12 (end of month 6 to end of month 12) ?

Analysis
Interest on sterling money-market loans and investments is calculated on
an actual/365 day basis. Lending £1,000 now for terms of three months,
six months, nine months and 12 months would yield the following
returns.

3 months $\quad £1,000 \times \left[1 + \left(\frac{6.0}{100} \times \frac{92}{365} \right) \right] = \quad £1,015.1233$

6 months $\quad £1,000 \times \left[1 + \left(\frac{6.5}{100} \times \frac{181}{365} \right) \right] = \quad £1,032.2329$

9 months $\quad £1,000 \times \left[1 + \left(\frac{7.0}{100} \times \frac{273}{365} \right) \right] = \quad £1,052.3562$

12 months $£1,000 \times \left[1 + \left(\frac{7.25}{100} \times \frac{365}{365} \right) \right] = \quad £1,072.5000$

End month 3 to end month 9

	£
End value	1,052.3562
Initial loan	1,015.1233
Interest earned	37.2329

$$R = \frac{£37.2329}{£1,015.1233} \times \frac{365}{(273-92)} = 7.40\% \text{ per annum}$$

End month 6 to end month 12

	£
End value	1,072.5000
Initial loan	1,032.2329
Interest earned	40.2671

$$R = \frac{£40.2671}{£1,032.2329} \times \frac{365}{(365-181)} = 7.74\% \text{ per annum.}$$

Current (spot) interest rates imply a rise in six-month interest rates over the next six months because the six-month forward/forward rate at the end of month 3 is 7.40%, whereas the six-month forward/forward rate at the end of month 6 is higher, at 7.74%.

Implications of Forward/Forward Rates

Because it is possible to imply what the market expects interest rates to be in the future, two important questions can be asked by analyzing current rates.

- Do market expectations usually turn out to be correct?
- If not, why is the analysis of implied future interest rates important?

Market expectations about future interest rates are by no means always correct. In the previous example for instance, it is quite possible that six-month interest rates will not rise, and the implied six-month rates of 7.40% after three months and 7.74% after six months will not occur.

Forward/forward interest rates are nevertheless very important because they allow banks to create and sell derivative instruments such as FRAs, interest-rate futures and interest-rate swaps. Banks can use current cash market or spot interest rates and instruments to create interest-rate instruments that apply to a time in the future, without risk to themselves.

Example
A bank can use the money markets to borrow in dollars at 6% for six months (182 days) and lend at 5.75% for three months (91 days). A customer of the bank would like to fix an interest rate now for borrowing for a three-month period, starting three months from now, i.e. from month 4 to month 6.

The forward/forward rate for months 4 to 6 is calculated as follows:

$$R = \frac{\$15.80}{\$1,014.53} \times \frac{360}{91} = 6.16\%$$

Time Diagram

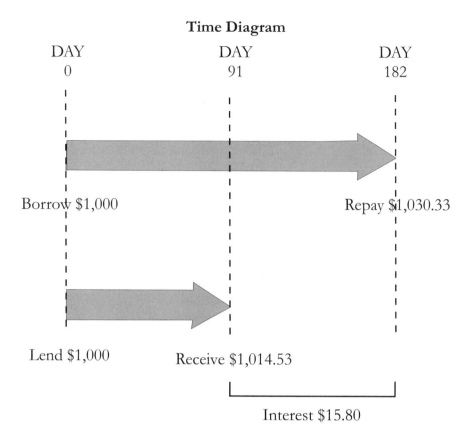

DAY 0   DAY 91   DAY 182

Borrow $1,000   Repay $1,030.33

Lend $1,000   Receive $1,014.53

Interest $15.80

If the bank agrees to lend money to the customer for three months, from month 4 to month 6, by quoting a rate just above 6.16%, it will be able to secure a certain profit. In other words, the bank can exploit current money market rates to fix a rate for future lending (or investing), certain in the knowledge that its activities should earn a profit.

Conclusion

The ability of banks to deal in instruments that fix an interest rate at some time in the future depends on a liquid market for cash instruments, i.e. a liquid money market for short-term rates and a liquid bond market for long-term rates. Without liquid cash markets, trading in derivatives becomes much more risky for derivative markets participants.

It is also important that there should be almost risk-free instruments in the market because the interest rates on these instruments set a benchmark for everything else that is traded in the market. Interbank loans and deposits between prime banks (at a rate that can be defined as LIBOR) and government bonds are such risk-free instruments.

Forward/Forward Rates and the Derivatives Markets

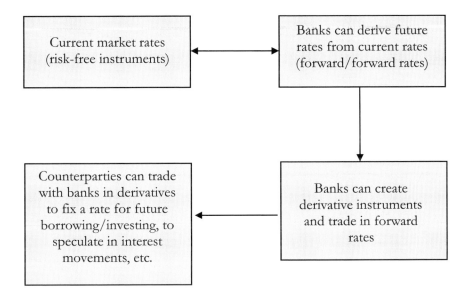

7

Basis Risk and Gap Exposure

Basis risk and gap exposure are two further aspects of interest-rate risk facing financial institutions, particularly banks.

Basis Risk

Basis risk arises when funds are borrowed on one interest rate basis and lent or invested on a different basis.

Basis risk involves changes in the pattern of interest rates. The pattern of interest rates refers to the relationship or the differences between interest rates on different types of financial instrument. For example, the basis for a three-month interest rate might be the interest rate on 91-day Treasury bills, or the rate on three-month Certificate of Deposit, or a three-month LIBOR rate in the interbank market. Basis risk occurs whenever the basis on which money is borrowed or received as deposits, differs from the basis on which the money is invested or re-lent.

Example
A bank lends £8 million to a company for three months at 1% above LIBOR and has funded the loan by issuing three-month Certificates of Deposit (CDs). Three-month LIBOR is 6.75% and the rate on three-month CDs is 6.625%. In three months' time, the bank expects to rollover the loan and the CD for a further three months. However, when the loan and CD are rolled over, interest rates have changed. LIBOR has fallen by 0.25%, the interest payable on CDs also has fallen, but by only 0.1875%.

Analysis

Basis risk exists because the bank is borrowing on one basis (the three-month CD rate) and lending on another. For the first three-month period, the profit margin is fixed because the bank borrows at 6.625% and lends at 7.75%, giving a profit margin of 1.125% (125 basis points) or £22,500 (1.125% of £8 million x 3/12).

Basis risk occurs because of uncertainty about future changes in the different interest rates relative to each other. After three months, the CD rate is down to 6.4375% and LIBOR is 6.5%, so that the bank's profit for this three-month period, lending at LIBOR plus 1%, will be just 1.0625% (7.5% - 6.4375%) or £21,250 (1.0625 of £8 million x 3/12).

The fall in the bank's profit margin by 0.0625% per annum (6.25 basis points) has reduced profit by £1,250 for the three-month period on the funding and re-lending transaction.

Basis risk may be greater when a bank borrows or lends at an interest rate related to its base rate and lends or borrows at an interest rate related to LIBOR. This is because the base rate is an administered rate that can change periodically in response to changes in market interest rates, whereas LIBOR is a market rate that is changing continually.

Example

A bank borrows £10 million at three-month LIBOR of 6.125% and re-lends at base rate plus 3%. It expects to rollover the loan in three months' time. Over the full six-month period, the base rate is unchanged at 6%. However, when the bank's loan is rolled over, three-month LIBOR has increased to 6.25%.

Analysis

The higher cost of borrowing in the second three-month period reduces the bank's profit for that period by 0.125% p.a. (12.5 basis points) or £3,125 (0.125% x £10 million x 3/12). This is because base rate is unchanged, and borrowers pay at a rate of 9% per annum over the full six-month period.

Basis risk is not usually significant for non-bank companies, although very large companies that borrow heavily and also invest surplus cash would be faced with some basis risk.

Gap Exposure

Gap exposure occurs when borrowing or lending is at a variable rate of interest on the same basis, but with a time difference between reset dates for the borrowing and lending. The exposure arises from the timing of the resetting of interest rates at the rollover period because interest rates might change in the interim.

Gap exposures are relevant to banks and other financial institutions involved in providing short-term finance or rollover (floating rate) finance. For example, a bank might lend $20 million at 50 basis points above three-month dollar LIBOR and finance this lending by borrowing $20 million at six-month dollar LIBOR. There is no basis risk because borrowing and re-lending are both related to dollar LIBOR. However, gap exposure exists because the interest rate on lending is altered every three months and on the borrowing only every six months. For example, a fall of 75 basis points in LIBOR would turn the profit of 50 basis points into a loss of 25 basis points per annum for three months on the borrowing and re-lending operation. The bank would be receiving 75 basis points less for three months while paying a higher rate on its own funds.

Example
A bank borrows £10 million at six-month LIBOR, and rolls over the loan at the end of six months and again at the end of one year. It uses the money borrowed to re-lend to a customer at three-month LIBOR plus 1%. The customer has this loan for 18 months.

Interest rates during this period were:

	Three-month LIBOR	Six-month LIBOR
	%	%
Start of period	7.50	7.625
End of month 3	6.50	Not applicable
End of month 6	6.00	6.125
End of month 9	5.50	Not applicable
End of month 12	5.25	5.625
End of month 15	5.00	Not applicable

Analysis

When the loan periods began, the bank was making a profit of 87.5 basis points p.a. (8.50% - 7.625%). The bank has a gap exposure, in this case to the falling trend in LIBOR. Actual profits over the eighteen-month period were lower than the bank might have anticipated and the hoped-for profit margin of 87.5 basis points is achieved only in the first three months of each six-month borrowing period.

Period	Lending rate (3 month LIBOR plus 1%)	Borrowing rate	Profit margin (basis points)	Profit/(loss) on loans of £10 million
	%	%		£
Months 1-3	8.50	7.625	87.5	21,875
Months 4-6	7.50	7.625	- 12.5	(3,125)
Months 7-9	7.00	6.125	87.5	21,875
Months 10-12	6.50	6.125	37.5	9,375
Months 13-15	6.25	5.625	87.5	21,875
Months 16-18	6.00	5.625	37.5	9,375
Actual profit				81,250

If the gap exposure had not existed total profits over the period would have been £21,875 per quarter (87.5 basis points or 7/8 % p.a.) or £131,250 in total for the 18-month lending term.

Gap Analysis

Gap exposure arises from the risk of adverse changes in interest rates between the time that a payment is made for borrowed funds and the time that interest is earned from the loans or investments made with those funds. *Gap analysis* is an approach to assessing the interest-rate risk from gap exposures by comparing periodically principal amounts of maturing assets (loans and investments) and liabilities (debts), and their interest-rate bases.

Example

Suppose that three-month sterling LIBOR is 8% and six-month LIBOR is 8.25%. The implied forward/forward rate for three-month LIBOR in three months' time is therefore 8.33% (workings not shown).

A bank might be considering whether to obtain funds at six-month LIBOR, at a cost of 8.25% p.a. in order to provide rollover finance to a customer at LIBOR plus 10 basis points with three-monthly reset dates for the interest. There would be gap exposure because the bank would be borrowing with six-monthly reset dates and re-lending with three-monthly reset dates.

The forward yield curve would show the bank what the minimum three-month LIBOR rate would have to be three months from now (the next reset date for the loan to the customer) if the bank is to at least break even on its borrowing and re-lending operation.

Suppose that the next three-month period is 91 days and the next six-month period is 182 days. If the bank borrows £1 million for six months at 8.25%, the interest cost will be:

$$£1,000,000 \quad \times \quad \frac{8.25}{100} \quad \times \quad \frac{182}{365} \quad = \quad £41,136.99$$

If the bank lends £1 million for three months at 8.10% (three-month LIBOR plus 10 basis points) the interest earned in the first three-month period will be:

$$\text{£1,000,000} \quad \times \quad \frac{8.10}{100} \quad \times \quad \frac{91}{365} \quad = \quad \text{£20,194.52}$$

After three months, the bank would have £1,020,194.52, as the original loan plus interest. To break even on its borrowing and re-lending, it must be able to lend this amount for the next three months to earn £1,041,136.99 that would be just sufficient to pay back its six-month borrowing with interest. This means that the minimum interest required in the second three months on the £1,020,194.52 is £20,942.47 (£1,041,136.99 – £1,020,194.52).

Therefore the minimum interest rate required from lending for the second three months is:

$$\frac{\text{£20,942.47}}{\text{£1,020,194.52}} \quad \times \quad \frac{365}{(182 - 91)} \quad \times \quad 100 \quad = \quad 8.23\%$$

If the bank can re-lend in three months' time for a further three months at LIBOR plus 10 basis points, the breakeven position is that three-month LIBOR at the reset date in three months' time must be 8.13% (8.23% - 0.10%). This compares with the forward/forward rate of 8.33%.

This example should illustrate the potential value of gap analysis for banks and other financial institutions, re-emphasizing perhaps the significance of forward/forward rate calculations in the money markets.

Funding Mismatches

A mismatch can occur between assets yielding a fixed rate of interest and variable-rate liabilities, or between assets yielding a variable rate of interest and fixed-rate liabilities. These are particularly relevant to banks that must control such mismatches to stabilize their profitability.

A potential recipe for disaster for financial institutions is to borrow short and lend long, where a lender funds a long-term loan with short-term deposits. This was the primary cause of troubles in the US savings and loan industry in the mid-1980s. Savings and loan institutions were financing long-term fixed-rate mortgages out of short-term floating-rate borrowings. In the event, interest rates rose and the short-term funding costs increased to more than the fixed-rate income from mortgages, and a number of savings and loan organizations got into severe financial difficulties. UK building societies and mortgage banks have avoided similar problems because long-term mortgages in the UK are at floating rates linked to short-term interest rates, and therefore broadly in line with the cost of their retail deposit base.

Example
A bank borrows £100 million at three-month LIBOR and lends to a range of corporate clients at fixed rates for two- to five-year periods. Lending is at an average margin of 300 basis points over LIBOR.

Analysis
There is a mismatch between the fixed-rate assets and variable-rate liabilities. If interest rates rose, the bank's profits on its lending operations would decline. If interest rates were to go up far enough, the bank's profits might be wiped out entirely.

Suppose there is a large increase in interest rates, and during a 12-month period LIBOR rises from 5% to 8.5%. With term loans fixed at 8% (5% + 500 basis points), the bank would incur a loss of 0.5% (50 basis points) or £500,000 per annum on its £100 million loan portfolio.

Commercial banks should avoid excessive exposures to such risks through their risk-management control systems.

The Currency of Borrowing

Companies can borrow readily in a variety of freely convertible currencies. The eurocurrency markets trade in loans and deposits in currencies that include the dollar, yen, euro, Swiss franc, sterling and Canadian dollar.

Interest rates are higher in some currencies than in others, and companies can choose to borrow in a currency with a lower interest rate. For example, a UK company might be tempted to borrow in euros if the interest rate is significantly lower on the euro than on sterling, and convert the euros it has borrowed into sterling by selling the euros in exchange for sterling. Interest payments and the eventual repayment of the debt would be in euros; therefore unless the UK company earns sufficient income in euros, it would have to buy euros at the appropriate time to make the interest payments and debt repayment.

However, a company should not fall into the trap of believing that currency borrowing must be cheaper if the interest rate is lower than the interest rate on a domestic currency loan. By borrowing in a foreign currency there is a risk that the full cost might prove higher than by borrowing at a higher interest rate in domestic currency.

For example, if the sterling interest rate is 8% and the dollar interest rate is 6%, it might be tempting to borrow in dollars to obtain a lower interest rate. A UK company might borrow $420,000 and, if the rate of exchange is £1 = $1.50 when the loan is obtained, sell the dollars to raise £280,000. The dollar loan would have been converted into sterling, but the company would be liable to pay interest and repay the loan principal in dollars. It would be at risk to sterling weakening against the dollar over the loan period, thus increasing the cost of buying dollars to make payments on the loan. For example, if the exchange rate were £1 = $1.40 when the loan had to be repaid, the cost of the repayment would be £300,000 ($420,000 ÷ $1.40), over 7% more than the original value in sterling of the loan.

The interest-rate differential in this example of 2% (8% - 6%) between sterling and the dollar would reflect the eurocurrency market's view of the likely change in the sterling/dollar exchange rate over the loan period. This can be explained as the re-alignment risk between the two currencies. When sterling interest is 8% and dollar interest is 6%, sterling will be perceived as a weaker currency, and at risk of falling in value against the dollar over the interest period.

The market's judgment might be incorrect, and sterling could weaken by more or less than expected over the period. Nevertheless, a company that borrows in one currency to invest in another is exposing itself to realignment risk.

Realignment risk can be summarized as:

- Borrowing in a foreign currency with a lower interest rate will be cheaper than borrowing in domestic currency provided that there is no change in the exchange rate over the loan period.
- However, currency borrowing can be more expensive if interest rates go up in the currency during the term of the loan and the loan is at a variable rate, and also if the currency of the loan strengthens against the borrower's domestic currency during the loan period.

Example
A company wishing to borrow £2 million for one year is informed by its bank that it could borrow at three-month dollar LIBOR plus 100 basis points (1%). Three-month dollar LIBOR currently is 5.5% p.a. and the exchange rate is £1 = $1.60. Alternatively, the company could borrow at 100 basis points over three-month sterling LIBOR, currently at 6.5% p.a.

There is no change in interest rates during the year, but the dollar rate against sterling changes as follows:

End of month 3	$1.59
End of month 6	$1.57
End of month 9	$1.55
End of month 12	$1.54

Analysis

Borrowing in sterling would incur interest at 7.5% (LIBOR plus 1%), totalling £150,000 for the year.

The company could borrow at 6.5% in dollars, and by borrowing $3,200,000 could convert the loan into the required amount of sterling (at £1 = $1.60). If the dollars required to pay the interest charges and repay the loan were purchased at the spot rate, the cost of the dollar loan would be:

Month	Item	Dollar amount ($)	Exchange rate	Sterling cost £	£
3	Interest	52,000*	1.59		32,704
6	Interest	52,000	1.57		33,121
9	Interest	52,000	1.55		33,548
12	Interest	52,000	1.54		33,766
12	Interest cost in sterling				133,139
	Loan repayment	3,200,000	1.54	2,077,922	
	Less original sterling value of loan			2,000,000	
	Exchange loss on loan repayment				77,922
	Total cost of dollar loan				211,061

$*^3/_{12}$ x 6.5% x ($3.2 m)

Although interest payments cost less on the dollar loan (£133,139 compared with £150,000) the overall cost of the dollar loan includes an exchange loss on repayment because the loan costs £77,922 more to repay than its original value. The total cost of the dollar loan therefore is £61,061 higher than borrowing in sterling. The borrower has suffered from the realignment risk that has eroded the interest-rate advantage of the dollar borrowing.

Hedging the Realignment Risk

A company could reduce or eliminate the realignment risk of an appreciation in the value of the currency with the lower interest rate. This can be done with *forward exchange contracts*. Briefly, a forward exchange contract is an agreement between a bank and its customer for the future purchase or sale of a quantity of one currency in exchange for another, at a rate of exchange and for a settlement date that are fixed in the contract. The exchange rate in a forward contract is different from the spot rate at the time the contract is made. The difference between the forward rate and the spot rate reflects interest-rate differentials between the two currencies. As a consequence, if a company

- borrows in a currency with a lower interest rate,
- converts the loan into a domestic currency, and
- arranges forward contracts to fix the exchange rate for buying the currency to make interest payments and the loan repayment,

it will end up no better or worse off than if it were to have borrowed at a higher rate in its domestic currency.

Example
Returning to the example on page 89, suppose the company borrows $3,200,000 at 6.5% (dollar LIBOR plus 1%), converts the dollars at £1 = $1.60 into £2,000,000 and arranges forward contracts to buy dollars for the loan payments. Available forward rates at the starting date of the loan are:

Spot rate	£1 = $1.6000
3 months forward	£1 = $1.5960
6 months forward	£1 = $1.5923
9 months forward	£1 = $1.5889
12 months forward	£1 = $1.5850

The loan payments will be approximately $52,000 in interest at the end of months 3, 6, 9 and 12 plus the loan repayment of $3,200,000 at the end of month 12. The company arranges forward contracts at these rates to buy $52,000 at the end of months 3, 6, and 9, and to buy $3,252,000 at the end of month 12.

Analysis
The loan repayments would be:

Month	Item	Dollar amount ($)	Exchange rate	Sterling cost £	£
3	Interest	52,000	1.5960		32,581
6	Interest	52,000	1.5923		32,657
9	Interest	52,000	1.5889		32,727
12	Interest	52,000	1.5850		32,805
12	Interest cost in sterling				130,770
	Loan repayment	3,200,000	1.5850	2,018,927	
	Less original sterling value of loan			2,000,000	
	Exchange loss on loan repayment				18,927
	Total cost of dollar loan				149,697

The cost of the dollar loan is almost the same as the cost of the sterling loan would have been (£150,000) because arranging forward contracts to remove the currency realignment risk also eliminates the advantage of borrowing in the currency with the lower interest rates.

Opportunities to Exploit Interest-Rate Differences

Normally lower interest rates on currency borrowing do not mean cheaper finance costs. However, if currency exposures were fully hedged, a multinational company with significant assets in two countries might be able to take advantage of interest-rate differentials between the currencies of those countries by

- borrowing in the currency with the lower interest rate
- investing the surplus funds at a profit in the currency that offers a higher interest rate.

The company would be deliberately grossing up its balance sheet with extra borrowings, but could make a profit without exposure to significant currency risk. This is because the loan payments can be paid out of normal trading income in the currency of the loan while the income in the other currency is reinvested at the higher rate.

Example
Some years ago a multinational company with sizable assets in both the US and the UK, appears to have adopted such an approach by borrowing in dollars and investing in sterling at a positive spread of up to 300-400 basis points. In other words, interest income was 3% to 4% higher on its sterling investments than the interest cost on its dollar borrowings.

At one stage, the company's reported consolidated accounts showed the following information on assets and liabilities by currency:

	UK £m	US (Sterling equivalent of $) £m	Total £m
Cash at bank	6,425	453	6,878
Short-term liabilities			
- Bank loans and overdrafts	1,799	242	2,041
Long-term liabilities			
- Bank loans	1,159	2,679	3,838

About one-half of the group's bank borrowings were dollar-denominated at a time when dollar interest rates were much lower than sterling rates, while over 90% of its cash on deposit with banks was held in sterling that gave a higher interest yield than dollar deposits.

The company's huge dollar assets and trading income meant that it could pay interest on its dollar loans out of dollar income, so that it could exploit the favorable interest-rate differential to borrow in dollars and invest for a higher yield in sterling, its reporting currency.

Large multinational companies are in the position of having extensive trading interests in two or more countries. Companies without this advantage would not be able to exploit interest-rate differentials between currencies in the same way.

Summary

Borrowing in a foreign currency in order to invest in domestic currency could be more costly than borrowing in domestic currency, even when the interest rate is much lower. If the borrower does not hedge the realignment risk by means of forward exchange contracts, the cheaper method of borrowing, in domestic or a foreign currency, will depend on the movement in the rate of exchange over the loan period.

Price Risk

Many banks trade in interest-rate sensitive securities, such as bonds and bills, and many investment institutions are large investors in these securities. Organizations that hold securities whose market value is susceptible to interest-rate movements are exposed to price risk. This is the risk of losses from an adverse movement in the price of investments caused by an adverse movement in interest rates.

Bond Prices and Interest Rates

The market value of a bond is the amount that investors currently are willing to pay to receive the future income stream from the bond. The future income stream consists of regular interest payments and the repayment of the debt principal at maturity. The current value or present value of this future income stream to a bond investor depends on the interest yield that the investor requires.

The market value of a bond therefore can be calculated by discounting the future interest payments on the bond and the principal repayment at maturity to a present value, using the required interest yield of bond investors as the discount rate.

It is not the purpose of this text to explain bond pricing in detail. However, the nature of price risk cannot be understood without an appreciation of bond pricing.

Example
An 8% bond has three years to redemption. Interest is payable every six

months, and the next payment is due six months from now. The current market yield on bonds with a three-year maturity is 8.6%.

Analysis

The market price of the bond can be calculated by converting the future interest payments and the principal repayment at maturity to a present value. We can calculate the value of bonds with a face value of 100. Because the coupon rate of interest is 8%, payable every six months, interest on bonds with a face value of 100 will be 4 every six months (8 per annum).

Each future payment of interest to maturity should be discounted to a present value. The discount factor to apply to each interest payment, and to the principal repayment at maturity, is:

$$\frac{1}{(1 + r)^n}$$

Where:

- r is the six-monthly yield on the bond, expressed as a proportion. For example, 5% would be 0.05, and 7.5% would be 0.075
- n is the number of interest payment periods to elapse before the payment occurs.

The annual interest yield required by bond investors on three-year bonds currently is 8.6%. For simplicity, we will assume that the six-monthly yield is exactly one half of this, 4.3%. Because the discount rate is 4.3% for six-monthly cash flows, the value of (1 + r) in this example is 1.043.

The market value of the bond is calculated as follows:

Date	n =	Item	Amount	Discount factor	Present value
After 6 months	1	Interest	4	$\dfrac{1}{(1.043)^1}$	3.84
After 1 year	2	Interest	4	$\dfrac{1}{(1.043)^2}$	3.68
After 18 months	3	Interest	4	$\dfrac{1}{(1.043)^3}$	3.53
After 2 years	4	Interest	4	$\dfrac{1}{(1.043)^4}$	3.38
After 2½ years	5	Interest	4	$\dfrac{1}{(1.043)^5}$	3.24
After 3 years	6	Interest	4	$\dfrac{1}{(1.043)^6}$	3.11
After 3 years	6	Capital repayment	100	$\dfrac{1}{(1.043)^6}$	77.46
Bond price					98.24

The bond will be priced at 98.24 per 100 nominal value. Of this price, 77.46 arises from the value of the principal repayment in three years, and the rest arises from the value of the remaining interest payments on the bond up to maturity.

Instead of saying that the price of a bond is the present value of future receipts to maturity, discounted at the yield required by bond investors, we can also say that, given the current price of the bond, it follows that the current yield required by bondholders is the discount rate that equates the current market value of the bond with the future income stream from the bond. In the example above, we can say that a price of 98.24 is equivalent to the future interest payments and debt principal repayment on the bond to maturity, discounted at 4.3% for each six months. It follows therefore that the yield to investors on the bond is 4.3% every six months, 8.6% per annum.

In other words, we can say either:

- a bond price can be calculated, given the yield required by investors; or
- the yield required by investors on a bond can be calculated, given the current market price of the bond.

Interest Rate Changes and Bond Prices

When interest rates change, the yield required by bond investors will change, and so bond prices will change.

- When interest rates rise or are expected to rise, required yields will go up and bond prices will fall.
- When interest rates fall or are expected to fall, required yields will go down and bond prices will rise.

Fixed Coupon Bond Prices and Movements in Interest Rates

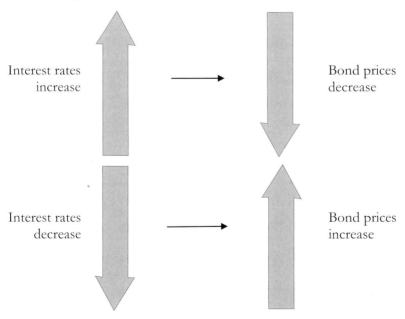

Interest rates increase → Bond prices decrease

Interest rates decrease → Bond prices increase

Example
Returning to the previous example, suppose that interest yields on three-year bonds go up from 8.6% to 9%.

Analysis
If we assume for simplicity that an annual yield of 9% represents a yield of exactly half (4.5%) every six months, the market price of the bond can be computed as follows, with $(1 + r)$ now (1.045).

Date	n =	Item	Amount	Discount factor	Present value
After 6 months	1	Interest	4	$\dfrac{1}{(1.045)^1}$	3.83
After 1 year	2	Interest	4	$\dfrac{1}{(1.045)^2}$	3.66
After 18 months	3	Interest	4	$\dfrac{1}{(1.045)^3}$	3.51
After 2 years	4	Interest	4	$\dfrac{1}{(1.045)^4}$	3.35
After 2½ years	5	Interest	4	$\dfrac{1}{(1.045)^5}$	3.21
After 3 years	6	Interest	4	$\dfrac{1}{(1.045)^6}$	3.07
After 3 years	6	Capital repayment	100	$\dfrac{1}{(1.045)^6}$	76.79
Bond price					97.42

Following the rise in bond yields from 8.6% to 9%, the bond price will fall from 98.24 to 97.42.

Managing Price Risk

For institutions that hold large quantities of bonds, managing price risk could be an essential requirement. One technique for *monitoring* price risk is to measure the *duration* of a bond or a bond portfolio.

Duration measures the price volatility of a bond in response to a change in the market rate of interest. To understand duration, it is useful to begin by looking at the concept of *futurity* and the maturity of a bond.

Futurity

The futurity of a bond is a measurement of how long on average an investor must wait to earn the interest and loan principal (on redemption) from a bond. A bond with ten years to maturity, for example, will have a longer futurity than a bond with just two years to maturity.

The futurity of a bond, unless the bond earns no interest at all up to maturity, i.e. unless it is a zero coupon bond, will be shorter than the remaining time to maturity. For example, the futurity of a ten-year bond will be less than ten years because although the debt principal will not be repaid for ten years, there will be payments of interest before then at regular intervals up to maturity. The *average* time the investor has to wait for his income therefore is less than ten years.

Futurity can differ for bonds with the same remaining term to maturity.

Example
Three different sterling bonds each have four years remaining to maturity, but have different coupon rates of interest. Interest is paid annually in each case. The expected cash returns to investors over this four-year period are:

	Year 1	Year 2	Year 3	Year 4	Total returns
	£	£	£	£	£
Bond A	0	0	0	100	100
Bond B	10	10	10	110	140
Bond C	20	20	20	120	180

Bond A is a zero coupon bond. The coupon rates on Bonds B and C are 10% and 20% respectively.

Analysis
Although these bonds have the same remaining term of four years to maturity, the cash returns to investors have a different profile or spread in each case. The Bond A investor must wait until the end of Year 4 for any return. For Bond B, interest at 10% is receivable at the end of each of Years 1, 2 and 3, representing 30/140 of the total returns from the bond to be received before the end of Year 4. For Bond C, interest at 20% is receivable at the end of each of Years 1, 2 and 3, representing 60/180 of the total returns from the bond to be received before the end of Year 4.

The average time an investor has to wait for the returns is greatest for bond A, the zero coupon bond, and least for Bond C. This average time of waiting is the bond's futurity.

Measuring Futurity
One method of measuring futurity is to calculate for each bond a weighted average of the time periods, i.e. the weighted average number of years the investor must wait for the cash returns. End-of-Year-1 returns can be given a weighting of 1, end-of-Year-2 returns a weighting of 2, end-of-Year-3 returns a weighting of three, and so on.

The weighted average can be shown by the following formula

$$\text{Futurity} = \frac{(R_1 \times 1) + (R_2 \times 2) + (R_3 \times 3) + \dots + (R_n \times n)}{R_1 + R_2 + R_3 + \dots + R_n}$$

Where:

R_1, R_2, R_3 are cash returns to the bond investor at the end of periods 1, 2, 3 and so on up to maturity at the end of period n, $(R_1 + R_2 + R_3 + \ldots + R_n)$ therefore represents the total income from the bonds to maturity.

Example
Using the example above, the futurity of each bond can be calculated:

Bond A $\qquad \dfrac{0(1) + 0(2) + 0(3) + 100(4)}{0 + 0 + 0 + 100} \qquad = \qquad \dfrac{400}{100} = 4$ years

Bond B $\qquad \dfrac{10(1) + 10(2) + 10(3) + 110(4)}{10 + 10 + 10 + 110} \qquad = \qquad \dfrac{500}{400} = 3.57$ years

Bond C $\qquad \dfrac{20(1) + 20(2) + 20(3) + 120(4)}{20 + 20 + 20 + 120} \qquad = \qquad \dfrac{600}{180} = 3.33$ years

These measurements show that the average waiting period for returns is a full four years for Bond A, less for Bond B and least for the high-interest Bond C.

Macaulay's Duration
A weakness of this measurement of futurity is that the weightings give equal value to returns in each year to maturity. Because money has a time value, and income received can be reinvested to earn more income, cash receipts in earlier years have more value, pound for pound or dollar for dollar, than cash receipts in later years. This time value of money can be allowed for by discounting a bond's future cash flows in each time period to a present value.

The discounted value (present value) of a future return is:

$$\frac{R_n}{(1 + i)^n}$$

Where:

Rn is the cash return at the end of period n

i, the rate of discount per period, is the current redemption yield on the bond.

A measure of futurity that incorporates present values is known as Macaulay's Duration. The formula is:

$$\text{Duration} = \frac{\dfrac{(R_1 \times 1)}{(1+i)^1} + \dfrac{(R_2 \times 2)}{(1+i)^2} + \dfrac{(R_3 \times 3)}{(1+i)^3} + \ldots + \dfrac{(R_n \times n)}{(1+i)^n}}{\dfrac{R_1}{(1+i)^1} + \dfrac{R_2}{(1+i)^2} + \dfrac{R_3}{(1+i)^3} + \ldots + \dfrac{R_n}{(1+i)^n}}$$

The weightings below the line in the formula must be at discounted values, just like the values above the line. The total value of the items below the line is the *total present value of future cash flows from the bond.*

Example

In the example above, suppose the current yield on all three bonds is 8% per annum. The measurements of duration for Bonds A, B and C will be:

Year	Discount factor, 8%	Bond A		Bond B		Bond C	
		Cash flow £	Present value £	Cash flow £	Present value £	Cash flow £	Present value £
1	$1/(1.08)^1$	0	0.00	10	9.26	20	18.52
2	$1/(1.08)^2$	0	0.00	10	8.57	20	17.15
3	$1/(1.08)^3$	0	0.00	10	7.94	20	15.88
4	$1/(1.08)^4$	100	73.50	110	80.85	120	88.20
			73.50		106.62		139.75

Macaulay's Duration for each bond is now calculated as:

Bond A $\dfrac{(0 \times 1) + (0 \times 2) + (0 \times 3) + (73.50 \times 4)}{73.50} = 4.0 \text{ years}$

Bond B $\dfrac{(9.26 \times 1) + (8.57 \times 2) + (7.94 \times 3) + (80.85 \times 4)}{106.62} = 3.5 \text{ years}$

$$\text{Bond C} \quad \frac{(18.52 \text{ x } 1) + (17.15 \text{ x } 2) + (15.88 \text{ x } 3) + (88.20 \text{ x } 4)}{139.75} = 3.24 \text{ years}$$

Once again, as with the previous calculations of the futurity of these bonds:

- the duration of the zero coupon bond, Bond A, is longest, and its duration is equal to the remaining term to maturity for the bond
- the duration is longer for Bond B and longest for the bond paying the highest rate of interest, Bond C.

This example of duration uses bonds with an annual interest payment. Duration also can be calculated for bonds where interest is paid semi-annually. The discount factor, i.e. the redemption yield, uses the yield for every six months, rather than an annual rate of yield, but the same basic formula is applied as illustrated above.

Duration and Price Volatility of Bonds

A significant feature of duration to bond investors is that the price volatility of bonds, in response to a change in the market rate of interest on the bond, varies directly with the duration of the bond. Duration therefore is a measure for assessing the price sensitivity of a bond to interest-rate changes.

The mathematical proof of this relationship is beyond the scope of this text, but the formula showing the relationship is:

$$\frac{\Delta P}{\Delta i} = \frac{-D\,P}{(1 + i)}$$

Where
Δ means a change in
P is the price of the bond
i is the market rate of interest on the bond
D is the measurement of duration for the bond (Macaulay's Duration).

Modified duration

For simplicity, investors and banks use a measurement of modified duration rather than Macaulay's Duration. Modified Duration, Dm, is:

$$D_m = \frac{D}{(1 + i)}$$

Because

$$\frac{\Delta P}{\Delta i} = \frac{-D\,P}{(1 + i)}$$

$$\frac{\Delta P}{\Delta i} = D_m\,P$$

Therefore $\Delta P = -D_m\,P\Delta i$

What this shows is that for a given change in the interest rate Δi, there will be a change in the price of the bond ΔP. This change is calculated by multiplying the change in the interest rate by minus the modified duration ($- D_m$) and the current bond price P. The minus sign shows that if there is an increase in i, there will be a fall in the bond price, and if the interest rate falls (the change is negative) the change in the bond price will be positive, i.e. the bond price will go up.

Example

The duration of a bond, as measured by Macaulay's Duration, is 4.60 years. The current yield on the bond is 9% per annum, and the current market price of the bond is 102.25.

By how much will the bond price change if the current market yield on the bond changes to:

- 9.1%, i.e. there is an increase in the yield by 0.1% or 10 basis points
- 8.85%, i.e. there is a fall in the interest rate by 0.15% or 15 basis points?

Analysis

Modified duration is derived from Macaulay's Duration, as follows:

$$D_m = \frac{4.60}{1.09} = 4.22 \text{ years}$$

Interest rate goes up to 9.10%

Change in price $= (- 4.22) (102.25) (0.0010) = - 0.43$.

The bond price will fall by 0.43, from 102.25 to 101.82.

Interest rate falls to 8.85%

Change in price $= (- 4.22) (102.25) (- 0.0015) = + 0.65$.

The bond price will rise by 0.65, from 102.25 to 102.90.

It is worth noting that the change in the bond's price, for a given change in interest rate, will be larger for bonds with a longer duration.

An important assumption, however, is that the duration (and modified duration) of a bond is the same at all price levels. In practise, it has been found that the modified duration for a bond is roughly constant over a fairly wide range of interest rates. Therefore the assumption of a constant value for duration, at the current interest rate, is sufficiently accurate. However, if interest yields change significantly, the duration of bonds also will change.

Exercise

A bond has a current price of 102.33. Its current redemption yield is 8.9% and its modified duration is 3.14.

If interest rates were to go up by 10 basis points, so that investors would require a yield of 9%, by how much would the bond price change?

Solution

The fall in price resulting from an increase of 0.0010% in the yield would be:

$(- 3.14) (102.33) (0.0010) = - 0.32$

The price would fall by 0.32 to 102.01.

Duration of a Portfolio

The duration of a portfolio of bonds is the weighted average of the durations of all the bonds in the portfolio, weighted for the relative value of investments in each bond in the portfolio.

Example
An investor's portfolio consists of 50% of Bond A, 25% of Bond B and 25% of Bond C. The durations of Bonds A, B and C are five years, ten years and seven years respectively.

Therefore the duration of the portfolio of bonds is:

	Proportion of portfolio		Duration (years)		Weighted average
A	0.50	x	5	=	2.50
B	0.25	x	10	=	2.50
C	0.25	x	7	=	1.75
					6.75

A target duration for an investment portfolio can be achieved by mixing bonds of different durations in suitable proportions so as to achieve the desired target.

Conclusion

Measuring the duration of a bond or a portfolio of bonds gives bondholders valuable information about price risk. Methods of hedging price risk, based on duration, have been developed. These techniques include immunizing a bond portfolio against interest-rate changes. However, a description of hedging techniques is beyond the scope of this book.

Risk Management

To manage interest-rate risk, an organization must monitor continually its exposures. Information should be gathered about borrowings and interest-bearing investments or loans, in particular the total amount borrowed or invested, the mix between fixed and floating rate, the term structure of loans and investments and their currency or currencies of denomination. Banks also should monitor their basis risk and gap exposures.

A company might have views about future movements in the general level of interest rates, likely changes in the yield curve, or movements in the exchange rate for a currency in which it has borrowing or interest-yielding investments.

Assessing Interest-Rate Exposures

Senior financial management should review continually:

- the total amount of borrowing or interest-yielding investments, and whether this is too high or too low in view of the current level of interest rates and likely movements in the future
- the desirability of changing the mix between fixed and floating-rate investments
- the need to change the term structure of the company's loans or investments
- the desirability of borrowing or investing in different currencies.

A bank should review whether measures are needed to reduce the basis risk to which the bank is exposed, or to reduce gap exposures.

The Need for Risk Management

Financial risk management by non-bank companies has tended to concentrate more on foreign currency exposures than interest-rate exposures. Losses on foreign exchange are reported in a company's annual report and accounts, and therefore are more visible. Losses from interest-rate changes are viewed as an opportunity cost and in general do not appear in published accounts, although losses from falls in the value of investments, possibly due to adverse interest-rate changes, are reported.

The scale of potential losses from adverse interest-rate movements can be very high for a heavily indebted company. A company's need to manage interest-rate exposure arises for two reasons:

- the volatility of interest rates
- the practise of fulfilling a significant proportion of funding requirements by short-term and long-term borrowing rather by than issuing shares.

Funding by Borrowing Rather than Equity
Many companies are funded largely by debt capital that is mostly variable-rate borrowing. Companies might prefer to raise capital by borrowing rather than by increasing equity through new issues of shares. When interest rates are low, borrowing might seem cheaper than equity finance, particularly as interest costs are an allowable expense item for tax purposes, whereas dividends on stocks are not. If banks are eager to lend, many companies are likely to become highly geared. (Gearing is defined as the proportion of a company's debt capital to its equity capital.)

High gearing (high debts relative to equity finance) can create substantial financial risks. The main danger lies with the high annual interest costs. A company has to make large profits simply to repay the interest it owes. In extreme cases, a company may not generate sufficient profit to pay the interest costs. Furthermore, loans are contractual obligations between the bank and the borrower. Similarly, a bond issuer has contractual liabilities to bondholders. Bank loans and bonds may have covenants, a breach of which would result in an event of default. For example, a bank-loan covenant might require a company to make sufficient profits before interest and tax to cover interest charges by a minimum multiple of twice the interest payments. Alternatively, a company might covenant to keep its debt/equity ratio below a maximum level of 1.5 : 1.0, i.e. debt not to exceed 150 per cent of shareholders' funds. If profit margins are squeezed in an economic downturn or recession, a heavily indebted company could face action by a bank or bondholder as a result of an event of default.

A further risk is that when market interest rates are high and volatile, companies may find it difficult to borrow at fixed rates of interest. If borrowing has been short-term and at variable rates, the company may be uncertain about future interest costs and whether it will be possible to obtain refinancing when existing loans mature (refinancing risk).

Recent Experience
Many large companies have debts in a variety of currencies valued at several billions of dollars. Large debts, high interest rates and low profit margins, can cause financing difficulties. Problems in the loans market and the bond market recur periodically. At the start of the new millennium, much attention has focused on heavily indebted telecommunications companies. Several of these borrowed heavily in 1999 and 2000 to fund the purchase of third-generation mobile telephone licenses in Europe. A number of factors, including fears of a slowdown in the world economy and reduced expectations for the speed of growth in third-generation mobile telephony, affected confidence and profitability in the industry. The most heavily indebted

telecommunications companies had to consider selling off parts of their business in order to ease their financial/debt problems.

The experience of companies in the telecommunications industry is just one example among many of the adverse consequences of interest-rate risk.

Example

Delta borrowed $200 million for five years at a variable rate of three-month dollar LIBOR plus 200 basis points, for a property-development project. The project was expected to yield a total return of $35 million on the eventual disposal of the property. When the loan was arranged and development work began, three-month LIBOR was 6% and the company assumed that this would be the average rate for LIBOR over the full term of the loan. Its expected interest costs therefore were $8 million ($20 million x 8% x 5 years). With development costs of $20 million plus interest charges of $8 million, total anticipated costs were $28 million, giving an overall expected profit of $7 million ($35 million - $28 million), or 25% on the cost.

However, suppose that interest rates rose sharply over the five-year development period, and the average three-month LIBOR rate was not 6%, but 9%.

Analysis

The actual interest costs would be $11 million rather than the $8 million expected ($20 million x 11% x 5 years). The total cost of the project would be $31 million, and the profit just $4 million, not much more than half the amount of profit originally expected.

An Approach to Interest-Rate Risk Management

The concerns of non-financial companies for the management of interest-rate risk will vary according to the extent that the company relies on debt funding.

Interest-rate risk can be reduced simply by borrowing less, or by putting less money into interest-bearing investments. When real interest rates are high, indebted companies probably will reduce their reliance on debt capital, and try to refinance their business by issuing new shares to pay off the debt. When real interest rates are low, however, the attractions of debt capital to borrowers and lenders will return.

Financial companies, both banks and investing institutions, have continual interest-rate exposures. For banks in particular, these can be very substantial.

When exposures to risk are high, there is likely to be a greater need for measures to limit or control them. Such measures include a variety of financial instruments that have been developed within the past ten to 20 years such as interest-rate options, forward-rate agreements, interest-rate futures and swaps. In addition, techniques for analyzing and evaluating risk within banks have become very sophisticated in recent years, and risk management within banks is a well-established practise.

A conceptual approach to risk management is summarized opposite.

An Approach to Managing Interest-Rate Risk

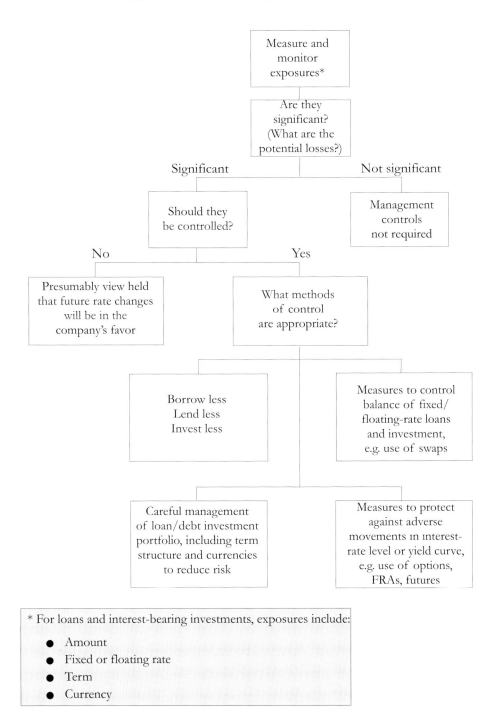

* For loans and interest-bearing investments, exposures include:
- Amount
- Fixed or floating rate
- Term
- Currency

Footnote on Interest- Rate Conventions

Throughout this text, the mathematical computations have made some simplifying assumptions about the way in which interest rates are calculated. In order to avoid possible misconceptions about this, a brief note is given below about the different conventions that are used to calculate interest rates.

Coupon and Interest-Rate Conventions

Coupon is a term used for the rate of interest payable on the face value of a bond. Bonds are issued at either a fixed rate of interest or at a floating rate.

- Fixed-rate eurobonds pay interest annually in arrears, on the anniversary of the bond issue. Some domestic fixed-rate bonds such as government bonds or gilts in the UK, pay interest every six months.
- Floating-rate bonds pay interest at a specified margin, in basis points, above a benchmark rate of interest, typically every quarter or every six months. The interest rate for an interest period usually is determined on the day before the interest period starts by reference to the selected benchmark rate at a specified time of the day.

Interest-payment dates are on the same day number in each payment month. For example, floating-rate notes paying interest quarterly might pay interest on the 21 February, 21 May, 21 August and 21 November each year. Because a payment date might fall on a non-working day, the terms and conditions of a bond issue will provide for payment of interest on the next business day after or possibly before.

Interest-Rate Conventions

Surprisingly perhaps, there are different ways of calculating interest on a debt. These different ways are known as interest-rate conventions and the terms and conditions of a bond issue must specify which interest rate convention will be applied to calculating interest on the bonds.

The broad rule for calculating interest for any period is that the interest payable shall be:

$$\frac{\text{Number of days in the period}}{\text{Number of days in the year}} \quad \text{x} \quad \text{Annual rate of interest (\%)}$$

The different interest-rate conventions define the number of days in a period or the number of days in a year differently.

- **Actual/365 basis**. This takes the actual number of calendar days in the interest period, and assumes a year of 365 days. This convention is used for sterling-denominated debt.
- **Actual/360 basis**. This takes the actual number of calendar days in the interest period, and assumes a year of 360 days. This convention is used in the money markets, e.g. the interbank markets for most currencies, including the dollar and the euro. Normally it is used to calculate interest on floating-rate notes in most currencies also, but not sterling.
- **360/360 basis**. This assumes that every month consists of 30 days, and a year has 360 days. Interest payable each month therefore is the same, regardless of the number of calendar days in the month. This convention was used on most eurobond issues in European currencies up to January 1999. It is used for US bonds also.
- **Actual/Actual basis**. This might appear to mean that interest

is calculated by taking the actual number of calendar days in the period and the actual number of calendar days in the year. Oddly, this is not necessarily the case, and there are different definitions of what Actual/Actual means. The ISMA definition that is applied to euro-denominated eurobonds issued since January 1999 takes:

$$\frac{\text{Calendar days in the period}}{(\text{Calendar days in the period}) \times (\text{Number of interest periods in one year})}$$

Example

Suppose that interest on a debt of £1,000,000 is payable at 8% per annum, and that interest is payable every six months for the periods 12 August to 11 February and 12 February to 11 August.

For a six-month period 12 August to 11 February (184 calendar days), the interest payable would depend on the interest-rate convention used, as follows:

Actual/365 basis: $£1,000,000 \times \dfrac{184}{365} \times 8\% = £40,328.77$

Actual/360 basis: $£1,000,000 \times \dfrac{184}{360} \times 8\% = £40,888.89$

360/360 basis: $£1,000,000 \times \dfrac{180}{360} \times 8\% = £40,000.00$

Actual/Actual basis $£1,000,000 \times \dfrac{184}{(184 \times 2)} \times 8\% = £40,000.00$
(ISMA definition)

Glossary

Arbitrage

Dealing in two or more markets at the same time, or in two or more similar products in the same market, to take advantage of temporary mispricing and make a certain profit on the dealing.

Assignment

The sale of a debt (receivable). Also the sale of a swap to a new counterparty, or the buyout of a swap by a new counterparty.

Basis Point

One hundredth of one per cent (0.01%) 100 basis points therefore are equal to 1%.

Basis Risk

The risk that interest rates on one type of financial instrument, e.g. Certificates of Deposit, will become less favorable in comparison to interest rates on another type of financial instrument, e.g. interbank lending. *See also Gap Exposure.*

Benchmark Rate

A rate of interest in the financial market against which other interest rates are set. A significant change in a benchmark rate will prompt changes in other interest rates. For example, in countries such as the US and UK, a change in the interest rate at which the government or government agency will deal in repo transactions (sale and repurchase transactions) in government bonds leads to immediate changes in all other money-market rates.

Bund
German government bond.

Commercial Risk
The risk of profits being affected by unexpected changes in trading conditions.

Coupon or Coupon Rate
Rate of interest payable on the nominal value of issued bonds or loan stock. For example, a dollar-denominated bond with a coupon of 5% will pay $5 interest per annum per $100 nominal value of bonds.

Credit Rating
Measurement of the creditworthiness of an organization with respect to loan stock it has issued. Large bond issues are given credit ratings, usually by two or more agencies such as Moody's and Standard & Poor's. The highest credit rating given to bonds by S & P is AAA (triple-A).

Duration
A measure of the weighted average time a bondholder must wait to receive the cash flows from a bond to maturity. The price sensitivity of a bond to changes in the bond yield can be measured using duration.

Eurocurrency
A convertible currency held in a bank account outside the currency's country of origin, e.g. eurodollars are dollars held in bank accounts outside the US.

Eurocurrency Markets
The money markets for lending and depositing eurocurrencies. Eurocurrency interest rates are comparable with domestic short-term interest rates in the currency's country.

Exposure
A financial risk facing a business that can be categorized according to its cause or source. Interest rate exposures are exposures to interest-rate risk.

Fed Funds rate

A key benchmark interest rate in the US. The rate at which the
government will lend money short-term to the commercial banking
system in the US. Changes in this rate will result in changes in all other
short-term dollar interest rates.

Financial risk

The risk of profits being affected by unexpected changes in financial
conditions or circumstances.

Fixed Rate

An interest rate that is set at the start of a transaction, e.g. loan, and does
not vary during the term of the transaction.

Floating Rate

An interest rate that is reset at predetermined intervals such as reset
dates or rollover dates, during the life of a transaction, e.g. a loan.

FRA

Forward rate agreement. A transaction used to fix an interest rate for a
future interest period. The concept underlying an FRA is that two
current interest rates can be used to fix an interest rate for a future
period. For example, the current three-month and five-month LIBOR
rates can be used to fix an interest rate for a two-month period starting
at the end of month 3 and ending at the end of month 5.

Future

An exchange-traded contract, in which one party buys an item from
another party through a futures exchange at a price agreed at the time
but for settlement or delivery at a future date. Interest-rate futures are
either short-term interest-rate futures (STIRs) or bond futures. The item
traded in a futures contract is a standardized item. For example, with a
bond future, the underlying item is a standard quantity of bonds.

Gap Exposure

Exposure to the risk of an adverse change in the interest rates on one
variable-rate instrument compared with another with the same

interest-rate basis, e.g. three-month LIBOR loan and six-month LIBOR loan. The exposure occurs in the time period between the reset date on one of the instruments and the reset date on the other.

Gilts
UK government bonds.

Government bond rate
The rate of return on fixed-rate loan stock issued by a country's government. The rate is a redemption yield – interest plus redemption value as an investment return on the current market value of the bond. Bond rates are quoted for different terms to maturity/redemption; for example 5-year bond yields, 7-year bond yields, and so on.

Hedging
Taking action to reduce or eliminate an exposure.

LIBID
London Interbank Bid Rate. Theoretically, the rate in the interbank money market at which banks will deposit funds with another bank with a high credit rating. LIBID typically is 1/8 of one per cent (12.5 basis points) below LIBOR.

LIBOR
London Interbank Offered Rate. Theoretically, the rate in the interbank money market at which a bank will lend to another bank with a high credit rating.

Maturity
The date in the future when a debt becomes repayable, or a bond is redeemable. Maturity is also used to refer to the remaining term to maturity of a financial instrument. For example, a bond with a three-year maturity has three years remaining until it will be redeemed by its issuer.

Present Value
A valuation in today's money of a future cash flow or a stream of future cash flows, after allowing for the cost of interest. Present value

calculations are based on the premise that $1 in a future year is worth less than $1 now because by investing less than $1 now an investor can obtain a return of $1 in the future year. Cash flows form an investment in future years that can be reduced to a present-value equivalent to assess the investment yield. Present-value calculations are the basis on which interest-rate investments are valued, i.e. they are used to derive market valuations.

Repo
Sale and repurchase agreement. A money-market transaction in which money is lent by one party against the collateral of high-quality bonds (government bonds).

Reset Date
A date on which the rate of interest on a variable-rate transaction, e.g. a loan, is adjusted, normally to a current market rate. The new rate is then applied to the transaction until the next reset date.

Rollover Date
See Reset Date.

Shorts
Bonds with less than five years to redemption.

Speculation (Interest-Rate Speculation)
Buying or selling currency in the expectation of movement in interest rates so as to make a profit, either in the same market or between two different markets, e.g. money markets and futures markets.

Swap
An interest-rate swap is an agreement in which two parties agree to exchange interest payments on a nominal sum of money at agreed intervals over an agreed period. In a fixed-floating interest-rate swap, one party might agree to pay interest every three months at a fixed rate of 6% in return for receiving interest on the same nominal sum at a variable rate, for example, six-month LIBOR. Interest-rate swaps have several

uses, such as managing interest-rate risk, and reducing the net cost of borrowing.

Undated Stock

Loan stock with no redemption date, and so a perpetual loan. Some government bonds or loans are undated.

US Prime Rate

The US equivalent of base rate in the UK. The benchmark rate of interest against which much corporate and personal bank borrowing and deposit rates are priced.

US Treasury Bonds

US government bonds.

Variable Rate

See Floating Rate.

Yield Curve

A term used to describe how current interest rates vary according to the term to maturity of the loan or deposit. When long-term interest rates are higher than short-term rates, the yield curve is upward-sloping or normal. When long-term interest rates are lower than short-term rates, the yield curve is inverse. These interest-rate comparisons can be shown on a graph; hence the term yield curve.

Zero coupon bond

A bond on which no interest is payable. It is redeemed at maturity at par. The current market value of a zero coupon bond is always below its par value, and will just reach par value only at maturity, when it is worth its redemption value.

Index

Notes

Notes

Notes

Notes

Notes

Notes